DISTINGTON

by

Les Nicholson

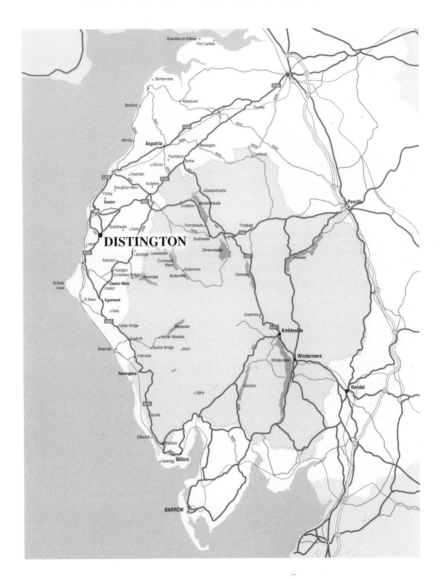

First published in 2008, ©Les Nicholson 2008

ISBN 978-0-9544112-3-7

Design, artwork and printing by Firpress Printers, Workington, Cumbria

CONTENTS

THE EARLY YEARS

Distington is one of the smallest parishes in the county, covering only about 3 square miles. There was plenty of coal and limestone which was extensively worked in its time. The earliest sign of life in the parish of Distington is the Druids Stone Circle at Studfold, near Pica. The stones can be seen in a small copse on the left-hand side of the road, when heading north, just past what was the Greyhound Inn. Erected in the Bronze Age, the 'circle' was an oval shaped ring, measuring 115 feet by 93 feet. A mound in the centre was excavated and found to be a burial mound, which had been robbed long ago. The chieftains of the local tribes would have been buried there. The circle was erected across the boundary lines between villages. It is still the boundary between the parishes of Distington and Dean today. The parishioners walked the boundary once a year to check that no ground had been lost to their neighbours, a forerunner of the Common Ridings that still take place in Scotland today.

The Romans came to the north of England in 87 AD and left 300 years later. In April, 2001, a hoard of Roman coins was found in the back garden of a house in Main St. A Distington man was digging in his garden when he found the Roman coins, buried in a leather purse. The village is on an old Roman road but there is no evidence of a Roman Settlement here. It is possible that the coins were buried for safe keeping by a soldier or traveller intending to return at a later date. The purse disintegrated when it dried out. The coins can be seen at the Roman Museum at Maryport.

The first village was Anglo-Saxon, dating from about 500 AD. One version of how the name was derived is DISS, probably the name of the chieftain, ING meaning clearing in a forest; the countryside was covered in trees in those days and TON, an Anglo-Saxon name for village. It seems to have become Distington sometime in the late middle ages. Another version is given in Bulmer's Directory of Cumberland, 1901. The name of Distington was said to be from the TON of Distingas. The early villages were built near water so it is probable that the first village was at Beck Green or Common End. Little is known from the Dark-Ages. Priests kept the only records and these were written in Latin.

At the time of the Norman Conquest, Cumberland was part of Scotland. The Norman 'Doomsday' book of 1086 shows that the border with Scotland was on a line from Millom to Middlesbrough. Cumberland was reclaimed from the Scots by William Rufus, son of William the Conqueror in 1092. Land was then given to Norman knights as a reward for their victory in the Battle of Hastings on 14th October 1066. In return, knights and landowners had to keep at least one horse and had to recruit local men to join the army when called upon by the King.

Early documentary evidence is of Gilbert of Dundraw, who was given the land in 1189. He lived in the parish in the reigns of Richard I (1189 to 1199) and King John (1199 to 1216). He was descended from Waltheof, Lord of Allerdale, and Odard de Logis, grandee of the manors of Wigton, Crofton and Dundraw. He had no son so his four daughters inherited the estate. In 1278, a part of the manor of Distington was conveyed to Thomas de Moresby and his wife Margaret. They lived in Moresby Hall, built by Morris, the Welshman, circa 1190. In 1487, the Manor passed into the ownership of the Dykes, and in 1578, it was held jointly by Leonard Dykes and William Fletcher, for homage and knight's services with a rent of 12 shilling 11 pence (65p) per year. Marriage between the families resulted in the Fletchers becoming the sole owners. After the death of the last of that family, it was sold by Decree of Chancery to John Brougham, Esq. of Scales (the first owner not to be knighted) in 1720.

In 1787, it was conveyed to Sir John Lowther, Baronet, who became the Earl of Lonsdale. The land had been let or leased out to different owners. The Earl of Lonsdale retained rights of the common lands only. These were enclosed by an Act of Parliament in 1768 with a share allotted to the church in lieu of tithes.

A stone castle, it was a Pele tower, from the old French word, 'pel' meaning stake or stockade. It was recorded in 1374 as Akehurst. The castle was built at Common End. It was built as a Norman Keep in the 12th century. It became known as Hay Castle in the 17th century, probably after the name of the land owner or the farmer living there at the time. It was originally the home of the Lords of Distington. It is now known as Hayes Castle.

It was a square building seventy feet (22 m) square with walls five feet (1.5 m) thick, had three floors and had a five feet wide moat surrounding it.

The tower would have had one door, built of thick and heavy oak timber, to withstand an attack. When these attacks occurred, the local villagers would round up their cattle and sheep and take them into the ground floor of the Castle. The villagers would then live on the second floor and the Lord and his family lived on the top floor. The Lords left the castle when they moved to Moresby Hall for a more comfortable life.

A typical Pele Tower, drawn by Emma Saville

A story says that Oliver Cromwell's army demolished the castle, because the Distington Lords had supported King Charles I during the Civil War rebellion, circa 1650, but other reports say that it was already a ruin before 1400. The castle in 1750 could still be recognised by its high walls and castellated roof line. A man, writing in a newspaper of the time, described it as a tasteless and mercenary Goth. He required some stones to build his farm, some stables and barns, so used the stones of the castle walls. Only part of the north wall is still standing now.

Distington was known as a township in the middle ages. It lies on the old Roman road from Bridgefoot. It is now on the A 595 trunk road from Carlisle to Barrow. The road is a straight road south from Bridgefoot, until it reaches Beck Green. The road then turns off the present main road (A 595), down the hill to a ford over the beck to continue towards Moresby Parks and Cleator. A packhorse bridge crosses the beck now. Packhorse bridges were built between 1620 and 1750. A track ran along the southern side of the beck from the bridge to Hayes Castle. The present road to Whitehaven was probably built when stage coaches came into use in 1688. When repairs were carried out on the road at Common End in 1965, over the beck to Hayes Castle, three bridges could be seen. The original packhorse bridge, the second at a higher level for stage-coaches and the third bridge brings the road up to today's level.

The base for the regular running for stagecoaches was at the Globe Hotel. They carried the mail to an office on the upper floor of the Queens Head pub. The steep hill up from the Boot pub was re-graded into an easier slope in 1965 to give traffic an easier climb when travelling north from the Boot. The bypass, known as the Loop Road, was opened in 1935. This road was also re-graded to reduce the slope of the steep hill. A new by-pass is now being built to take through traffic away from the village, due to be opened in December 2008.

At the north end of the village was Toll Bar cottage, where a gate closed the road to travellers heading north. This was before the road to High Harrington was built. When a fee was paid, the gates were opened to allow passage through. Villagers would often walk up to the gates when out for a stroll but turned around rather than pay the toll to pass through. The cottage stood where the new roundabout at the Harrington road junction is now. I remember there was a large tri-angular garden planted with vegetables looked after by the then resident, Tom Timmins. At the south end of the village was the common ground belonging to the village.

A description of the village main street in 1701 written by a past vicar, quoted in the Church Centenary book, said that the main street had many trees and had single storey houses, which then had thatched roofs. By 1801, the houses had two floors and also had slate tiles on the roof. Most of the trees had gone. It had many shops and tradesmen, many local farms and coal was extensively mined. The population in 1701 was 500. In 1901, the population had increased to 1,922, living in 386 houses, averaging less than five people per house. The number of houses included 90 in Pica, plus Gilgarran hamlet and all the farms. Gilgarran hamlet already existed long before William Walker built his mansion from 1805 to 1809 but much more development took place at this time. Pica was built when Oatlands Pit opened in 1886. In the 2001 census, there were 900 houses with 3,944 people living in the parish.

Some interesting, notable families have taken up residence in Distington in the past. The history of the Blakeney family was researched for a booklet produced for the Festival of Britain celebrations in 1951 by the late Alfred Scott, Headmaster of Distington Secondary Modern school.

Mr Scott recorded that the Blakeneys were well known in military life. Originally from Norfolk, John Blakeney came here in the 18th century. He was a Junior Ensign in the army and on 13th August 1704, he fought well and was made up to Lieutenant during the Duke of Marlborough's Battle of Blenheim. He was promoted to Captain in August 1709.

He retired from his unit, the Royal Regiment of Foot of Ireland and came to live in Distington. He lived in a large house known as Woodville, later known as the Black Cock Inn, which are now three private houses known as Woodville Cottages. He had paintings of George I and George II in his house. In his will, he specified where he wanted to be buried; three yards to the north of any other burial and to the west of the Church. This was prior to the present church being built. He died on the 21st May 1749, aged 68.

His nephew, George Augustus Blakeney, born 29th January 1716, was also in the army as a Lieutenant, promoted by the Earl of Harrington. He was later promoted by the Duke of Cumberland to Captain when fighting Bonnie Prince Charlie in the Jacobite rebellion of 1745. He went to Canada with General Wolf, who died at his moment of triumph in the capture of Quebec, aged just 32. George Blakeney retired after this. He had a portrait of Duke of Cumberland and a painting of the 'Death of Wolf' in his house. He died 25th February 1774, and was buried in the same tomb as John Blakeney. In turn, his grandson was the next to have had an army career before returning to Cumberland. He became 'Collector of Taxes' at Whitehaven and was made Deputy Lord Lieutenant of Cumberland by Lord Lonsdale. He died in his house at the corner of Cross St and Irish St Whitehaven, and was buried in the family vault in Distington Church. The next in line was Catherine, who never married and Thomas. Thomas deserted his ship in Quebec in 1821 and was never seen again. The last of the line was Robert Blakeney, JP, who died on 6th November 1882.

THE VILLAGE IN THE 19th CENTURY

The population of the village grew steadily through the years. In 1801, 721 were living here. In the following census reports, there were as follows:

1811 - 910 inhabitants 1821 - 988 inhabitants

1831 - 960 inhabitants 1841 - 1,108 inhabitants

1851 -1,106 inhabitants 1881 - 1,789 inhabitants

Shops, farms and pubs were the main businesses of the village. The three leading men in the parish in 1829 were Charles Fisher of Distington Hall, Captain James Robertson-Walker of Gilgarran and the Reverend Henry Lowther, Rector of the Parish and said to be the richest man in the village. Another Distington man became a well known poet. He was William H Armstrong, who died in 1841, aged 23.

In 1847, according to the Mannix and Whellan's Directory, Distington was a self supporting village. As well as a large number of farms and pits in the area, shops operated very well in the village. Among those listed were:

John Allison, shoemaker

Will Barwick, tailor

Matthew Bewley, blacksmith

Thomas Bewley, grocer, bacon supplier and farmer

James Borthwick, land agent for Curwen Estates,

Mrs Eleanor Bow, general merchant supplier

John Crosthwaite, another tailor.

Major Henry Caldecott of Prospect House was a well known businessman of the time.

A Turnpike barrier gate operated beside the Toll-Bar Cottage. Turnpikes first appeared circa 1730 and ended in the late 19th century but the cottage remained until the 1950s.

Terraced houses at this time included Pandora Terrace, named after a daughter of the Robertson-Walker family, Garrett's Row, Castle View, Bird Lane, Sunnybrow and Town Head. Castle View was on the main road to Whitehaven opposite Hayes Castle Road. These terraced houses were knocked down shortly after the Second World War. Garret's Row, adjacent to the Victoria Hall was knocked down circa 1950. Pandora Terrace still stands opposite Distington Motors garage and Town Head is opposite Millyard.

Mr Joseph Ritson Wallace (1805-1895) set up a museum. The specially designed building was built in 1875. It was described as in the style of a 'Rustic Doric' building, 40 feet long and 20 feet wide. (12m by 6m). There was a gallery on the upper floor with a geometrical spiral staircase around a 'Saracen' column, made by a Distington man, Robert Bell, a self taught architect. Mr Wallace, the owner, was a West Cumbrian, working as the owner and editor of the Manx Liberal, an Isle of Man newspaper. He spent little time here. The result was that it never opened on a regular basis. One room was full of Polynesian dresses, weapons and ornaments. Local specimens of rocks, etc. took up a large area. The museum was fully equipped by 1842. When the museum closed down, after the death of Mr Wallace, aged 90, everything was sold off. The exhibits totalled over 10,000 items and each was labelled by name. The building became private houses after this and is now called Museum Villas.

QUARRIES

A number of quarries were dug throughout the Parish. A lime quarry was dug and a kiln operated opposite the Church in 1874, where the Community Centre now stands. The quarry filled with water when it became disused and the field became known as the Pond Field. Others were dug and still working after 1850. They were at Stubsgill, Robin Hood, Barngill, Colingate in Gilgarran, and at the top of Pikey Hill (Pica). A quarry here was worked by J Bain & Company, a Glasgow Iron Maker, in 1883. The Company leased this quarry from the Fisher family and royalties were paid from 1883 to 1889.

A large quarry, known as Barffs Quarry, to the rear of Barffs Road, was dug when limestone was exported from Harrington harbour. Behind it were the Long Quarry and the Short Quarry as well as a number of other smaller quarries. The track from the church ran past Barffs quarry to Harrington and was called the Lime Road. The Fisher family of Distington Hall owned the quarries. Work stopped suddenly when the quarrymen turned up for work one morning and found that water had flooded into the quarry. This quarry was abandoned before 1880. All these quarries produced large amounts of red sandstone, white freestone, barley stone, millstones and stones for building work in the Parish.

Over many years, a number of people have lost their lives in the Barffs Quarry. In a report in the Whitehaven News on the 4th November 1927, Joshua Caruthers of Workington disappeared with his girl friend, Miss Mary Cowan of Salterbeck. Their bodies were found tied together in the quarry. An inquest was held in the Church Hall, Distington on 20th November 1927 and lasted from ten o'clock in the morning until four in the afternoon. The bodies were on display throughout the inquest.

Two schoolboys Colin Denwood and Tony Graham, playing beside the quarry in the late 1940s, reported seeing a woman's head floating in the water. When the Police Diving Team arrived, it was found to be a sheep's head.

WATER SUPPLY

On an 1874 O/S map, the fields around the village that had previously been named were now numbered. A number of wells were shown to be in Distington for the water supply. On the eastern side of Main Street, they were as follows: opposite the Queens Head Pub, in field 138, in the cellar of Hinnings House and in field 179, behind Hinnings House, owned by John Bewley, at the rear of Harriet's Home, in field 180, owned by John Richardson, rear of number 123 in field 184, owned by Gilgarran Estates and tenanted by Mr Kirkpatrick, rear of the Reading Room, in field 186, rear of The Lodge, in field 192, adjacent to the drive to Prospect House.

On the western side of Main Street, there was one on the path to Hinnings Farm, two wells in fields 127 and 162 at the present T-junction in Hinnings Road, near the Doctor's surgery. On Main Street, they were at the rear of number 94 in field 170 and at the rear of Rathbones CI in field 174 that used to be Myers & Bowman's yard.

Two wells were also in the fields opposite each row of terraced houses on Church Road, fitted with hand pumps in field 179, the Pond Field and field 132, rear of Queens Head Pub. Three new bungalows have now been built on the site of this well. At the Boot Bridge, there was a well at the Birkett's Brewery, Distington, later owned by Mr Dalzell of Parton Brewery, in field 247. All these wells show how much water lies under our village.

Twenty houses at Common Side, Common End were supplied from a well in the Old School Field, opposite Hayescastle Road. This well was known to be twenty feet deep. Four houses got their water from a stream fed from a spring in the fields of High House farm on the road from Pica towards Moresby. This stream passed through a wash room and a midden heap on the farm and flowed beside the road and under tunnels to emerge at Hayes Castle before

entering Distington Beck at Common End. There were many outbreaks of Dysentery and Scarlet Fever in this area in the 19th century.

Mr Garret and Tom Bramwell also fitted pumps to their wells in Main St. Offensive smells came from the sewers in Main St. Two water-troughs were in the village, one on the road to Hinnings Farm on Chapel Street and one at the junction of the main road and Beck Green.

By 1900, the water was piped into the village by Workington Corporation, fed from Crummock Lake. A reservoir was built at High Harrington, opposite the road to Lowca and was originally said to be filled from the springs of the Lamplugh fells. It was covered in and grassed over to look like a field. It was operated by the Joint Harrington and Ennerdale Water Board. The reservoir contains 188,000 gallons of water. Water is now supplied from Ennerdale Lake.

Gilgarran village was supplied by three springs before coming on to the mains supply, circa 1940. All three springs dried up after the opencast mining took place on Branthwaite Moor.

A surface water drain was laid through Main St, Distington from the northern end of the village. It was joined at the Queen's Head junction by the drain from Church Road and followed the road down to Beck Green and then across the green to Boot Bridge. Surface water can still be seen flowing when looking over the eastern side of the bridge.

Distington Beck, (Lowca Beck when it crosses the boundary) was described in a Record Office report by fishing expert, Izaak Walton in the early nineteenth century, as a small river with plenty of small trout in very clear water. This was before any work had started on the beck. The beck starts on the moors of Branthwaite. It then runs behind what was the High Duty Alloys factory. It fed into a reservoir by a mill race created when a weir was built to the north of the field behind Mill Yard. The reservoir fed the corn mill at Mill Yard. Crossing under the bridge on the Pica road, the beck meanders to Beck Green. A short distance north of Beck Green, another weir was built for the mill race to a saw-mill. It then crossed under the bridge at Beck Green to rejoin the beck on its way to Common End. A third weir was built at the rear of Wellington House, still there today. This millrace supplied the water to Castle Mill, on the site of Hayes Castle, another corn mill. The water wheel has rotted away over the years but the inside working machinery, made of wood is still in good condition. Another mill used the beck. This was the Harrington Mill, which stood across the boundary between Distington Parish and Harrington Parish.

A tributary from Stubsgill, Pica, flowed through Prospect Woods to join Distington Beck near Beck Green. A brick dam was built on the tributary just before it entered Prospect Wood. A large diameter cast-iron pipe can be seen coming from the dam to supply water to one of three suggested places. Prospect House once had a fountain in its garden and required a large supply of water to feed it. Another possible reason was to supply water to the railway line to Oatlands Pit. It was a steep climb from Distington and the steam powered railway engines needed a lot of water for the hard climb up to Oatlands Pit. A pit was dug beside the line because a plentiful supply of water was always needed for the steam engines. The third suggestion was that water was needed for a mill adjacent to Prospect House. This was Mr Smith's spade and edge tool mill and forge. If this was correct then why was the dam built to the east of Prospect Woods and not a weir close to the mill?

In 1886, the Moresby Coal Company started building three new rows of terraced houses on Whillimoor at a high and bleak area known as Pikey Hill, later called Pica. The miners worked in the new Oatlands Pit, which opened for trade in 1890. Ninety houses were built with another thirty being built later. The houses were built to a low standard. The water to these houses was to a single tap in the back yard. The water supply came from the Oatlands pit. Local farmer Robinson Burns started operating a horse drawn wagonette bus service from

the pit and Pica to Whitehaven. This continued on a regular timetable until CMS started their motorised bus service to the village in the 1920s.

Horse drawn coaches operated from the Queen's Head pub and the Globe Hotel Distington. The horse drawn buses left from Town Head (Millyard), leaving at 10.00 a.m. and 1.30pm on Thursdays and on Saturdays afternoons at 2pm and 6pm. They travelled to the Wheatsheaf pub in Whitehaven, return times being at 2.30 and 5pm on Thursdays and 4pm and 8.30pm on Saturdays. The charge was 9 pence equivalent to 3½ new pence, and 6 pence single, which is 2½ pence in today's money. To and from Howgate cost 6 pence and 3 pence single.

The Albert Hall was built at Common End, circa 1880, by the Birkett family of the Castle Inn. It faced up Swallow Hill. It was used as a dance hall, for functions and as a Reading Room. Newspapers could be read by the local people on a daily basis. A new Reading Room was built on Main Street and opened in 1901. Donations and a gift from the Robertson-Walker family paid for the building. It has also been used as the village library. It was sold to developers in 2007. In 1888, the Victoria Hall was built. The proprietor was Mrs Nancy Thompson, who was licensee of the Queens Head pub. The pub sold Bass beer at that time. The Hall was used for many activities, including dances, bird shows and indoor training for football teams, boxing matches and other events. It was also used as a canteen for school dinners after WW II.

The Coronation Hall stood behind the Globe Public House. This was originally called the Globe Assembly Rooms, run by Isaac Frear, pub landlord in 1884. It was another hall used for entertaining the public and for dances. After WW II, a professional touring group used to visit regularly, putting on concerts of popular wartime songs. The upper floor was used as a Catholic Church. It is now private houses.

The roads at this time were mostly mud and deeply rutted which was a problem in the dark. Sixteen oil lamps were erected in Main Street in 1895, lit each evening by John Kirkpatrick. Jonathon Crookdake of Pandora Terrace and Joseph Tolson, were both blacksmiths at the end of the century.

DISTINGTON HALL

Distington Hall was built for Benjamin Fisher, whose family were Whitehaven traders in 18th century by J Dixon, of Whitehaven. It was built with two floors, a cellar and an attic. It stood in its own grounds and was on the road to Gilgarran. The Crematorium now stands where the stables used to be. Grandson Charles Edward Fisher, who, died in 1883 was known as the Gentleman of the village. He became a JP and was a trustee of the village church. His wife, Ellen, died 4th July 1904. She had given £500 donation to the church, plus a stained glass window and the carved pulpit. She was also a Sunday school teacher. A plaque to her memory is in the church. The family bought the land from Lord Lowther and owned the large Barffs quarry, before it was abandoned.

The Fisher family connection with Distington started with Benjamin Fisher, born 9th February 1717, who married Bridget Draper, born 6th January 1716, on 21st April 1743. Their family comprised of Isobel, born 8th February 1744, Anthony, born 28th August 1748 and died 18th February 1749, aged 6 months, and Mary, born 18th November 1751 and died 27th April 1863, aged 92. Bridget died 27th April 1755, aged 39. Benjamin had a second marriage in Dublin to Mary Boucher on 24th May 1763. From this marriage, another four children were born. First was Elizabeth, born 2nd February and died 14 days later and next was Anne, born in Dublin on 17th July 1764. She died in Moresby Hall on 15th January 1845, aged 80. Then came another Benjamin Fisher junior, born 26th November 1766, in Dublin and also died in Moresby Hall on 5th September 1828, aged 43. William was born in the Hall on 6th August 1766 and died at sea on 24th October 1793 aged 24. Mary Fisher, nee Boucher died at Whitehaven. Benjamin Fisher senior, died at

Distington Hall Coat of Arms.

sea on 24th May 1786, aged 70.

A son, continuing the name Benjamin Fisher was born in Dublin on 26th November 1766 and married Jane Gibson at Moresby on 11th October 1791. Jane was born in Cockermouth on 11th July 1764. Their son, William Fisher was born in Moresby Hall (which seems to have become another family home) on 28th November 1793 and died in Liverpool on 1st August 1846, aged 53. Peter Fisher was born in Moresby Hall on 3rd April 1796. He died on 3rd April 1863. Another Benjamin Fisher was born in Moresby Hall on 1st April 1798. He was lost at sea in 1825. John Gibson Fisher was born in Moresby Hall on 21st May 1800 and died just 2 years old. Catherine Fisher was born in Moresby Hall on 15th March 1802. Another John Gibson Fisher was born in Moresby Hall on 25th July 1806 and also died, only 2 years old. Charles Edward died in 1883. Jane Fisher died at Moresby Hall on 11th September 1827, aged 63. Benjamin Fisher also died at Moresby Hall aged 63 on 5th September 1828.

Charles E Fisher had married Ellen Knobley, who died in 1904. Their family were Charles, born 1860, Edward and Peter. Edward married Florence, who died in 1942. Their family were Benita, Kathleen and Leslie. Peter married Anne Mary and their children were Edward, Benjamin, Dorothy, Peter, Nigel and Mary Ellen who was born in 1874 and died in 1910. Charles E Fisher sold some of his property in Crellin Street, Barrow in 1868 and the remainder in 1870. He then gave money to the West Cumberland Infirmary in Howgill Street, Whitehaven. In 1901 and 1904, Edward Fisher raised money to buy property in Oklahoma USA, as an investment. All this information is in a solicitor's letter at the reading of a will seen in the Record Office.

Royalties were paid to the Fisher family by J Bain and Company, an ironworks company, from 1883 to 1889. Limestone was quarried and taken down the track to Harrington harbour for exporting to Scotland. The track became known as the Lime Road. The quarry had to be abandoned when water flooded into the workings. The railway was built in front of the Hall and the Hematite Ironworks behind it. This made the family unhappy about the noise and smoke. They left the Hall to live in Carlton Lodge, Bedfordshire. It was left empty. A plaque was put in the church, as can be seen in the next chapter. The Hall was sold to the Distington Iron and Hematite works as offices in 1910. During World War II, the hall was used by the Home Guard, led by Lt Joe Rudd who used it as a base. The Home Guard patrolled from the Hall to the adjacent High Duty Alloys. They operated a guard post under the Dragonfly railway bridge. After the war, the Hall was allowed to fall into ruin and was demolished when the Crematorium was built. The Crematorium opened in the summer of 1974. The Lodge, home of the gatekeeper and standing at the bottom of the drive onto the Gilgarran road, is still there and is now in use as a private house.

Distington Hall

GILGARRAN MANSION

William Walker, a Whitehaven trader, and his sister, Anne, bought land at Gilgarran, a hamlet with a number of farms, from the Earl of Lonsdale. They started in 1805 to build a mansion, situated two miles from Distington station on the Cleator to Workington Junction railway. When it was completed in 1809 it had many rooms with the attic floor used for servant's quarters. A boiler for the heating of the building was in a large cellar, split into three sections, a wine cellar, boiler room with space for storing coal and coke and larders with ample space for storing goods. The mansion had its own gravity fed water supply from a spring at Frear Bank, Gilgarran, into a pit holding 4,000 gallons. In 1905, the system was extended to include Gilgarran hamlet and its farms and other buildings. In 1914, the sewage system was improved and was said to be satisfactory.

The mansion stood in 13 acres of what was described as a wilderness and improved to become good quality ground. There was a large amount of hardwood trees, such as spruce and larch. The estate had natural facilities for the breeding and rearing of game. Prior to 1914, the annual average was put at 800 pheasants, 50 brace of partridge, 50 woodcock, 40 hares and 900 pairs of rabbits. Many were trapped and shot. A considerable amount of money was spent on planting good cover.

Houses were built for the workers on the estate and the hamlet was developed. William and Anne travelled widely to collect plants and trees from home and abroad to improve the estate. In 1819, the mansion contained no paintings or works of art so the Walkers decided to go to Italy looking for items and paintings to improve the mansion. William was killed, aged 40, when their ship the Brunswick, was attacked by a Spanish gunship Pronte on 1st June 1819. After the attack, Anne Walker was brought back to her Gilgarran home on a Royal Navy Frigate, commanded by Captain James Robertson,

RN. Captain Robertson was born in Ross-shire, Scotland in 1783. He joined the Royal Navy in 1801 and had served as a Midshipman on Lord Nelson's ship, the Victory. James became captain of the Royal William in 1851 and after this appointment, he retired from the Royal Navy, aged 68.

With an agreement to take the Walker name, James and Anne married on 24th June 1824 and became the Robertson-Walkers. James was 41 and Anne was 43. They had a big influence on the parish and James became the village squire. The squire also became a Justice of the Peace, (JP) for many years, as did his descendants. James was appointed High Sheriff of Cumberland in 1844. Anne died 15th December 1854, aged 74. James Robertson-Walker then married his cousin Katherine Mackenzie, who was 37 years younger than him, in 1856. James died on 25th October 1858. Katherine erected a Celtic stone cross on his grave. She lived to be 72 years old and died in 1892. Both marriages were childless and a nephew, James Robertson was named as heir in the captain's will of 1852. The will stated that there should be no changes to the estate for 1,000 years.

Squire James was a gentleman of the old school. He lived in a grand style with a staff of seven maids, a butler, a groom, a coachman, six gardeners and five woodsmen. He also had a staff of seven working on Home Farm.

In 1874, he married Emily Austin of Kent and there were four children. The eldest was James Francis Austin, then Arthur Maxwell Murdo Robertson-Walker. He was killed in action during the First World War at the battle of the Somme in 1916. Their eldest daughter Anne married Lt General Sir Basil Hitchcock, KGB DSO Second daughter, Dorothy Emily Austin married Alan Napier, H M Consul to Venice and Naples.

Gilgarran Mansion, pictured front (above) and rear (below)

James Francis Austin Robertson-Walker inherited the estate in 1927 and was described by the rector as a fine Christian and a gentleman in every sense of the word. He married Ethel Margaret, daughter of Thomas Hardy of Armathwaite Hall in 1916 and died on 6th August 1940. They had two sons, Ian Maxwell Murdo and Austin Thomas Robertson-Walker. Ian inherited the mansion on the death of his father but lost his life when serving as Engineer Lieutenant on his ship, HMS Gloucester during the battle of Crete on 22nd May 1941, aged 21.

Austin Thomas succeeded him but two claims of death taxes in a short time meant the end of Gilgarran Mansion.

In the 1861 census, Gilgarran had 26 adults with 17 children living in the hamlet. Most of the adults worked for the Robertson-Walkers. In the 1881 census, the population had increased to 44 adults but there were only nine children.

In the early 19th Century, Katherine Robertson-Walker, the daughter of the next Captain Robertson-Walker married Mr Hugh Munro-McKenzie. They bought the 18th century Prospect Farm, a small farm in 1801, and developed it by 1830 into a large house. The house had an East and a West Wing. A large fountain stood in the gardens. In the 1847 Mannix and Whellan directory, Major Henry Caldecott owned Prospect House. The Roberson-Walker family built Belle View House, Swallow Hill, for a daughter and later, it was the home of Dr John Stanley, MD, a Whitehaven surgeon who operated in the Howgill St Hospital. On 21st March 1927, Captain James Robertson-Walker died.

An article in the Distington Parish magazine reported that a Garden Party was held on Friday 10th June 1932, starting at three o'clock in the afternoon and finishing in the evening. Volunteers were requested to help set up the stalls and more men came than were required. A collection was held and a good sum of money was donated to the church's Lay Reader's Fund.

The estate was put up for auction on 28th July 1921, because of the problem of previous death duties. The Lots to be sold were the Mansion and its grounds, along with the buildings belonging to the estate.

The Mansion was described as substantially built

with yellow freestone. It was approached by two carriage drives, one from Gilgarran Hamlet and the other on the road from Distington towards the Greyhound Inn. It had its own excellent water supply and was lit by acetylene gas. In the sales brochure issued by Mitchell's Auction Co. Ltd, it listed the ground floor as having an entrance hall, drawing room, dining room, library, smoke room, boudoir, business room and lavatory. On the West Wing, there was a large kitchen and well fitted scullery, housemaid's pantry, butler's pantry, servant's hall and a lavatory. The rooms on the first floor of the main building were four large bedrooms and a dressing room. On the East Wing were three bedrooms and a dressing room, with bathroom and lavatory. The West Wing had four bedrooms; store room with bathroom and a lavatory. The cellar was large, split into three sections, including a wine cellar, three larders and ample space for coal and coke for the fires and boiler. There was an ornamental conservatory, twenty four feet square, opening out of the library, heated from the cellar boiler. A large fountain stood in front of the Hall. The grounds covered thirteen acres and had been very carefully laid out and had a great variety of ornamental trees, evergreen shrubs and plants. There were two wired-in tennis courts, a croquet lawn and golf course in the grounds. A kitchen garden supplied nearly all of the vegetables required.

Also on the list was the gardener's cottage, agent's house, a cottage and gun room, chauffeur's house, dairy, joiner's shop, barn, gas house with acetylene generating plant, groom's cottage, stables, motor garage, laundry and wash house and an audit room. These were all in the hamlet of Gilgarran.

Other Lots were Tithe Barn Cottages, Gilgarran Home Farm and the woodlands around it, estate keeper's house and gamekeeper's house, Kelmore Hills Farm, Dyon Side Farm, Belle View House and grounds, Common Side Farm, High House Farm, Town Head Farm, Distington, and numerous fields and meadows throughout the local area. It appears that not much was sold as there was another auction later when the mansion was sold off when the family left the area. The family were again hit hard by death duties when first, Captain James Austin Robertson-Walker died on 6th August 1940, and his son Lt Ian Murdo Robertson-Walker, RN, died aged 21 when his ship was lost in action in the Mediterranean Sea on the 22nd May 1941 during

WW II. The surviving son, Austin Robertson-Walker, known as Tinto, became the next owner. Because of death duties, he moved out on the 2nd October 1951 and decided to sell the mansion.

The second auction took place on 28th April 1953. The mansion was sold with few changes from the original auction. Items such as a white marble fireplace, a black marble fireplace and mahogany panelled doors were sold separately as well as floorboards and lighting fittings. The main staircase was sold to a west Cumbrian garage. The carved stonework was sold in the last auction in October, 1953 and the mansion was not demolished until 1957. The sale raised £13,000. Tithe Barn House was sold to Mr and Mrs Dobie for £600. Mr Dobie had worked for many years as a chauffeur and Mrs Dobie worked as a maid for the Robertson-Walker family.

A new estate, Gilgarran Park was built by Lovell's and Co. Building work started in 1960.

THE CHURCH and CHAPELS

The church occupies a mound overlooking the village. It was stated in the book compiled to celebrate the Centenary of the church that a wooden church was on this site in the early Anglo-Saxon times, surrounded by an oval wooden fence. An Anglo-Saxon stone church probably stood here in a later period. Relics of old stonework and a stone cross were found when the foundations of the present church were dug.

A stone church was built by the Normans. The first Rector is recorded as Gilbert, son of Serlo, in 1178. Another church was built, circa 1330, dedicated to St Cuthbert. The church had two bells, now in the tower of the present church. One bell was cast 1394 or 1404, dedicated to St Cuthbert. It was one foot four inches in diameter and tuned to note 'C', weighing 1 cwt. It is said that when a bell was dedicated to St Cuthbert, it is probable that the body of St Cuthbert had lain in the church.

St Cuthbert died on 20th March 687 and was buried at Lindisfarne Priory but when the Vikings started raiding the area, the Monks of Lindisfarne carried his remains away for safety and did so from 875 to 894. The monks carrying his body may have rested in Distington church and also settled in various parts of Cumberland to keep ahead of the Vikings. The monks tried to cross the Duddon Estuary on their way to Ireland but got caught by the fast incoming tide and had to leave the lead-covered coffin in the sea overnight before recovering it the next morning. They then returned to West Cumberland. St Cuthbert was eventually buried in the new Durham Cathedral opened in 999 AD.

The second bell is thought to be older and is dedicated to St Christopher, the patron saint of travellers. This bell, tuned to 'B' flat, is one foot eleven inches in diameter and weighs one and three quarter cwt. Both bells were in the church of 1552 and are still in the church today.

The living in 1537 was reported to be £7-0-11d per year, equivalent to £7-05p in today's money, a large amount for those times. Most of this was in tithes from the parish, mainly sheep, cattle, corn and fish.

According to Whellan's History of Cumberland and Westmorland directory of 1860, St Cuthbert's church was built about 1660 but it may have been during the time of Oliver Cromwell, 1649 to 1658. A font in the church is dated 1602. It consisted of a knave, chancel, porch and a turret with two bells. The architecture both inside and outside the church was plain. The arch of the old church, dividing the chancel from the knave, was retained when the today's church was built. It still stands on the northern side of the church. Both the 1330 church and the 1660s church seem to have been given the same name.

The church records were written in Latin and first recorded in 1653. A priest wrote that a local man went far away to get a wife. He went to St Bees, a distance of six miles. A later priest held the living of the rectory for 61 years. The churchyard was oval until extended in1876. In 1917, the churchyard was extended again to its present size and a wall was built around it. This was all paid for by public subscription. The parish covered 3,065 acres; the glebe covered an area of 530 acres. This was land owned by the church and rented out to farmers.

Today's church is The Church of the Holy Spirit, replacing the old stone built St Cuthbert's church that was described by the church council as damp and had rotting timberwork. In November 1882, a decision was made to build a new church and a building committee was formed. The chairman was the Rev William Wentworth Wodehouse, secretary was the curate, Rev James Henry Latrobe Bateson, who was the driving force behind the project in 1883, and the treasurer was Mr Edward Dryden. The committee consisted of Hugh Munro

Mackenzie, who died in January, 1885, before the church was completed, church warden Henry Southward, John and James Robertson-Walker, and Robert Salkeld.

The firm of Hay and Henderson, Edinburgh, were appointed architects and Mr Cook was to be Clerk of Works. The contractor was W P Christopherson. When building work started, it was realised that Mr Cook was also the foreman for the contractors. He was replaced as Clerk of Works by James Davie. When the Rev. Wodehouse was absent, Mr John Munro Mackenzie took over as chairman.

Hugh Munro Mackenzie and his sister Mrs Katherine Robertson-Walker had each contributed £1,000 donations, along with many other donations including Charles E Fisher of Distington Hall who donated £500.

Building work started when the foundation stone was laid by Lady Lonsdale in June, 1883, with Mrs Robertson-Walker and Mrs Fisher of Distington Hall also attending. When building work started, Distington was in the Diocese of Chester. In 1885, this changed to the Diocese of Carlisle.

St Cuthbert's Church demolished 1886/7

Knave arch of St Cuthbert's Church

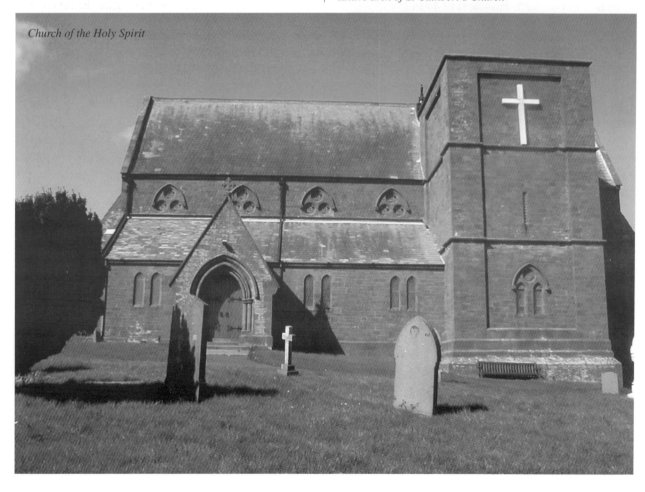

Church of the Holy Spirit

The church was built in Old English Gothic style. The main supporting columns are polished marble from Peterhead. The outside walls are of red limestone from Pica Quarry and the interior walls of white limestone are from Gilgarran Quarries. The church nave is 15 metres long by 5.35 metres wide. The aisles were 2.75 metres wide at each side. The chancel, also 5.35 metres wide, and is 9.9 metres long. The overall length is 25 metres long, 11 metres wide and the top of the roof is 15 metres high. The tower is 6.9 metres square and is 14 metres high. Some limestone from Fletcher's Quarry on the Barffs was also used. The two old bells were refitted into the new tower. The alter is three metres long and was carved from solid oak. The organ was fitted into the church in 1901. Before that, a piano from the old St Cuthbert's church may have been used. The Church of the Holy Sprit was consecrated on 25th November 1886, by the Bishop of Carlisle, Bishop Harvey Goodwin. At the time, it was called the 'Little Cathedral of the North'. The Bishop was not very complimentary about the outgoing Rector. Money for the building of the tower ran out and the donators refused to give any more. No explanation was given for this. The new Rector was Rev William G C Hodgson. He remained Rector until his death in 1914.

A monument was erected to Captain Robertson-Walker, who died on 6th November 1882. Plaques on the inside of the church walls are dedicated to Captain Arthur Murdo Maxwell Robertson-Walker, who was an Adjutant in the Battalion of the Royal Fusiliers, and also to Katherine Robertson-Walker of Gilgarran, who died 21st December 1892 age 72. Another monument was erected to Hugh Munro McKenzie, who died 30th January 1885. A memorial tablet was erected in the church and was dedicated to Robert Blakeney, who died on 6th November 1882 age 64.

Another tablet was placed in the church in 1920, honouring the dead of the First World War. There are 47 names on the tablet. The dead of the Second World War are marked by a plaque erected underneath the first one. Further plaques in the church commemorated Ellen Fisher, who died 4th July 1904 age 72 and for Duncan Robertson Napier, born 6th November 1871 and died 24th November 1898 aged 27.

There are three modern windows in the church. A window was dedicated to long serving church warden Herbert Wrangham, 1941 to 1956. Another window was dedicated to Mrs Ada Bowman in 1975 and a third window was dedicated to Stan Grant for his services to the church, which was erected by his family. He was churchwarden from 1978 to 1984. The lych-gate was erected in 1936 to commemorate the 50 years anniversary of the rebuilding of the church.

Queen Anne (1702-1714) set up a bounty to pay clergymen of the Church of England. A grant by Parliament in 1801 of £10 per year was given. Tithes, meaning 10 per cent, of all produce produced by parishioners was to be paid to the church. In the 18th century, this tithe for Distington Parish was paid to the Bishop of Chester. In 1840, it was decided that money would be paid instead of goods. These charges included every new cow, two pence each, every milk cow, halfpenny each, a swarm of bees, one penny, a goose, six pence and a hen was four pence. The tithes were commuted in 1846 but continued to be paid to the Bishop of Chester until 1869.

In 1893, the Rector was the Reverend William George Courtenay Hodgson MA, JP who was described as the Rector and Surrogate, Rural Dean of Whitehaven. The Reverend W C Thompson of Midtown was the curate. Before 1960, Church of England Rectors could control a number of churches and a vicar was employed by the Rector to run an individual church.

The tithes raised by some churches gave some Rectors thousands of pounds and made them very wealthy men. When this ruling was changed, the income went to the Diocese, and then Rectors and Vicars received a more balanced wage scale.

The old Parish Register, used from 1646 to 1729, was inscribed on vellum and was written mostly in Latin. They are now in the Diocesan Archives in Carlisle Cathedral.

A typical year was recorded in 1910 as having ten weddings, sixty one baptisms and forty three funerals in a population of 1,922 people living in 388 houses. The rateable value for that year was given as £7,467.

A Dedication Festival was held on Sunday 25th November 1928 when the Mothers' Union gave new curtains, said to be of chaste and beautiful design and cushions for the chancel. A new carpet, a gift from the Rector, the Reverend W Johnson was also dedicated.

The Church built a Sunday school on Church Road, adjacent to No 17 in 1787. It was reputed to be the first in Cumberland and maybe in England. This was replaced by another school built in 1836. It was a two-story building, one room on each floor. 346 children were enrolled in the early days, 198 from Distington, 130 from Pica and 18 from Gilgarran. After the Second World War, the building was used for two extra classrooms for the Main Street School. The Sunday School had a hall built on to the back of it in 1961, for use as a church hall. It was dedicated to John Bird. The Sunday school gradually became too expensive to maintain. It was demolished on 17th June 1993.

The old Rectory was where The Chestnuts is now. The Rectory was built between 1795 and 1800. It was described as a two-storey building with attic bedrooms and a cellar. The out-buildings consisted of a barn of five bays, a hen house, a swine house and stables for six horses. At that time, only the Rector in the village, who was a wealthy man, kept horses and a carriage and used them for travelling around the parish. The windows of the main room looked straight down the drive to the Main Street. Two large gates stood at the entrance on Main Street and a six foot high wall surrounded the grounds. There was an orchard and two gardens. Bee-hives were also kept. Many tall trees stood at the rear of the Rectory. Adjacent to these gates was a small stone built house, built for the gatekeeper. This was nicknamed 'Sparrow Castle'. In later times, it was used as an overnight lock-up for people who got too drunk to get home.

The Old Rectory. Photo Courtesy of Workington Library

In 1884, the Rector was Reverend Henry Lowther. He had a portrait of his mother painted by Sir Joshua Reynolds, along with other paintings of the Flemish School.

The Rectory was sold as a private residence in 1954 to a family called Nicholson (no relation) and sold again later to Jacky White of Gilgarran. The building was demolished, prior to houses in the Chestnuts being built in 1989. An earlier Rectory was at Prospect Villas on Main Street, now a private house. The present Rectory was built adjacent to the church in 1954. The Reverend A J Sowden was the first to live in the new rectory. He never lived in the old rectory; instead he lived in rented accommodation, 25 Pandora Terrace.

Pica had St Cuthbert's Mission, part of St Cuthbert's Church, which stood at the junction of the road to Distington. Their services started at 6:30pm each Sunday evening with a Sunday school at 2:00pm. The Mission Hall was built with tin sheeting walls and roof.

Mr Repson looked after St Cuthbert's Mission until he left in 1928. He was presented with a gold wristlet watch on the eve of his departure. The mothers of the scouts put on a feast for all to enjoy. Mr Repson went to study at a Missionary College in Essex, a good place for training in the Ministry.

In December, 1918, the Parish Council appointed a committee to erect a Memorial to the brave men who lost their lives during the Great War. A war memorial was erected on the road to Common End and was unveiled by Major C Valentine of Workington on 16th April 1921. The Memorial was then handed over to the Parish Council to be preserved for the future. It contained the names of the dead in the WW I. Other names were added after the end of WW II.

The Memorial committee consisted of Isaac Fox, chairman, with John W. Mitchell, Museum House and James Morton, Windscales who were joint secretaries, James Crone, Boot Inn, treasurer, and Thomas Wilson, Clerk of Works. Committee members were Samuel Somerville, Mill Cottages, John Messenger, Main Street, William Birkett, Woodside and Herbert Hunter of Pica.

A Wesleyan Chapel, a Primitive Methodist Chapel and a Presbyterian Mission Hall were also in the village. From 1745, Methodist preachers have passed through the village. The early preachers came to Whitehaven, which was part of the Newcastle circuit. This brought Charles Wesley to preach here in 1749, when on his first visit to West Cumberland. Hodgson Casson, a lay preacher, formed a plan to build a chapel. In 1829, Thomas Litt bought the land from the Curwen Estates and a chapel was built in 1830 on Main Street. The building has changed very little to this day. The first Trustees, with Thomas Litt were Daniel Douglas, Wilfred Wilson, Joseph Thompson, James Turner, William Loney, John Wilkinson, Hugh Williamson, John Rigg, John Armstrong. Jacob Sewell, Joseph Pape, George Hannah, James Smith, John Douglas, Joseph Cape and John Daykin. Among the many ministers was a well known man of the time, Dr Punshun in 1845/46. Distington had three lay-preachers at the time, Mr Armstrong, Mr Smallwood and Mr Gibson. Later two more men followed, Robert Roach and Robert Milling.

A Primitive Methodist Chapel was built in the middle of Boot Brow, Common End, in 1839.

Primitive Methodism has been practised since 1823. William Clownes with Hugh Bourne, the founder of Primitive Methodism, preached in Distington on Friday, 8th November, 1823, which was part of the Hull Circuit. Much of its early years involved a family called Sharpe. There were two sons, Joseph and John. One went to the USA and became a well-known minister. The other went to Australia and became famous there. Both returned to Distington in later life. The Chapel closed down for many years but reopened in 1874. John A Dixon started here and rose to become a preacher near Doncaster. The Harrison sisters served as Trustees for 40 years. The Wesleyan and Methodist Chapels merged in the 1960s. The Primitive Methodist Chapel at Common End closed down and was sold off to become a private house in 1989, converted by builder, Robert McCracken.

The Chapel at Common End was in the Workington district and the Main Street Chapel was in the Whitehaven district. The Presbyterian Chapel, with seating for 45 people was on Church Road and used by the Brethren.

COAL MINES

Coal was mined in Distington from 1614. The early pits were called bell-pits. They were named because of the shape of the working area and were not very deep, usually not more than 25 feet (8 metres). Others were drift mines with tunnels driven into the side of hills.

The Fletcher family of Hayes Castle were responsible for developing pits in 1614. They leased and then bought royalties for £20 in 1624 from John Fearon. In 1675, royalties were bought by Sir John Lowther for £53. He also bought royalties in 1699 for £60. In the latter part of the 17th Century, Christian and Thomas Lamplugh operated mines in this area. It was reported in his book 'West Cumberland Mining 1600-1982' by the late Oliver Wood that in 1714, Sir James Lowther bought and operated Gunnerdine Colliery in Distington. Gunnerdine Colliery was worked from 1693 to 1718 and yielded 6,582 tons in 1806. It was then used for short periods in 1728 and 1736. It was reopened in 1806 and between 1811 and 1814 and had an output of nearly 18,000 tons. Stubsgill Colliery was working in 1675.

Moresby Hall pit closed in 1738, Lister Pit closed in 1741 and Fisher Pit closed in 1750. There seems to be no information on when these pits opened. Blearbank Pit operated from 1771 to 1776. Barngill Pit was sunk before 1737. Lattera Pit operated from 1714 to 1731. Birkett's Pit, 1718 to 1723. Hall Pit and Quarter Pit were worked at this time. Jane Pit at Boonwood was working in 1731. The coal was shipped out through Parton harbour until the port closed down about 1720. There were five collieries named in 1737. A colliery was the name for a group of pits. For example, Harrington Colliery consisted of twelve pits. These collieries were named as Lattera, Birketts, Hall, Quarter Bank and Distington Colliery.

Mining continued in Distington through the 18th century. A pit was working at Boonwood in 1768. In 1781, Mr Allinson Crosthwaite owned Boonwood Pit and operated High Pit and Moss Pit on his own land. Royalties were paid to Lord Lonsdale. There was also Glaister pit, circa 1781. Barngill Pit was sunk before 1787. Lord Lonsdale continued working the Bottom Band Colliery until April 1865, when the coal seems to have become exhausted. He sank Dyon Pit in 1815 and worked this until 1851. The pit flooded in 1840, was pumped out and reopened the following year.

At Gilgarran, Captain Robertson-Walker operated his three pits from 1830 to 1838. These pits were taken over by Ralph Tate in 1843 and closed in 1854. Ralph Tate owned two more pits, Commonside Distington and the other was Castlerigg Pit. Another pit was at Spring Hill at Common End. He leased Hayes Castle Pit from 1863 to 1872. The coal was from a three foot seam at a depth of 78 feet (24 metres). Mr McKenzie and Mr Main reopened the old Yard Band Pit in Gilgarran and started a fourth pit in 1872. All were closed down by 1875.

Henry Curwen of Workington operated two pits. They were Annie Drift, Windscales and Whythemoor, both stated as being in the Distington Parish area.

The next pit was the Oatlands Pit at Pica, sunk to a depth of 108 fathoms (198 metres) in 1880 by the Moresby Coal Co. It opened for production in 1886. The pit employed 351 men in 1909. Average output from 1911 to 1920 was 821,000 tons per year. The pit was bought by the United Steel Company in 1924. Due to the years of the depression when money was scarce, the pit closed in 1932 and abandoned in 1934. The miners then had to walk to Walkmill Colliery Moresby, to start work at 6 am.

Opencast mining was the next coal mining activity. Coal at a shallow depth was dug out of poor moor land ground at Pica near the site of the old Oatlands Pit. This area was spread over 490 acres. In 1985, the site was extended towards Moresby Parks and Keekle. The site was in full action when the Distington History Society visited in 1997. When the work was finished in 1998, the site was filled in and landscaped to leave the ground in better condition than it was before work started.

RAILWAYS

Distington got a railway line when the Cleator to Workington Junction Railway Company, known as the C&WJRC, built a new line. Work was started in 1873. The railway tunnel at Bransty was becoming a bottleneck, causing trains to run late. Then the charges for using the tunnel doubled. The Earl of Lonsdale, of Whitehaven, Lord Leconfield of Cockermouth and Mr Henry Curwen of Workington decided to form a new company, the Cleator and Workington Joint Railway Company. The line was built through Distington and Moresby Parks. It opened to goods traffic in June 1875 and opened to passenger traffic on 1st October 1879. Three other lines were built into Distington Junction in the next two years. A line was built to Whitehaven, and owned by London and North Western Railway Company, running passed Barffs Quarry to Parton in 1879. This was a single track line, except at the bridge near to the church. A second track here had been laid to stand wagons for the loading of sandstone from the quarry. The line carried passengers from 1881 to 1883. It was then used to carry miners to and from Lowca pits. It reopened for one year only in 1913.

Another single track line was called the Gilgarran Branch. This line was also built by the London and North Western Railway Company, in competition with the Cleator and Workington Railway Company. It ran behind what later was the High Duty Alloys factory to Branthwaite and Ullock and on to the Marron Junction, on the Workington to Cockermouth line. This line never carried passenger traffic. When Distington Ironworks Company opened in 1879, they used this line to take out pig iron from the ironworks and brought in coal from Durham for the furnaces. Local coal was not used because it was a much higher grade of coal than was required. The line closed when Distington Ironworks closed down.

In August 1877, Glasgow iron makers, William Baird and Co, proposed a railway from Distington to Rowrah. By October it was approved and William Baird agreed to pay the first £500 in legal and parliamentary fees. The Bill received Royal assent on July 4th 1878. The builders, Robert Ward & Co of Carlisle were instructed to build the bridges wide enough for double track but bought land only for single track. By Christmas, a contract was given to Edgar & Murray Ltd, to build two stations, one at Oatlands Pit (Pica) and one at Arlecdon for a cost of £218-6s-7d. This line opened on 18th October 1879. The first passengers were carried on this line in 1883. The line became known as Baird's Line. When Distington Station was built, it had three platforms, a subway between platforms and a signal box which had 24 levers for controlling signals and points. It could be seen overlooking the main road. There was also a stone built engine shed. This shed stood beside the bridge which crossed over the road to Pica. The stationmaster was Mr John Holmes. For the first two years, the Furness Railway Company jointly operated the running of this line with its well-known maroon coloured engines and cream and maroon carriages. In August, 1884, the C&WJR bought their own engines. They purchased 0-6-0 saddle tank locomotives from the Lowca Engineering Co. This line closed to normal passenger traffic in 1935 but special trains still used the line. A train ran from Cleator Moor to Workington on football match days, workers travelled from Egremont to Sellafield and the Distington British Legion also used the line for a day trip to Seascale.

John Kelly worked from Distington Station as an agent for both the London and Northwest Railway and for the Furness Railway companies in 1901. The Baird line was closed to passenger traffic in April, 1931.

The line from Distington was a steep climb to Oatlands Pit. Engines struggled up the incline but loaded wagons were allowed to run down unconnected with men running alongside to control the speed. They must have been very fit men!

Baird's line closed in 1946. Iron-ore was carried from Rowrah to the ports, but this eventually stopped, not because the ore was worked out but because of excessive costs in royalties to landowners. The main Cleator to Workington line owned by British Railways since nationalisation on 1st Januaryn1948, closed in January 1970.

An Act of Parliament in 1892 amalgamated many local lines. This still caused the army a lot of trouble during WW I, so in another act in 1923, the four big railway companies were formed, namely, LMS – London Midland Scottish railway, LNER – London – North Eastern Railways, GWR – Great Western Railways and SR – Southern Railways. LMS took over all of Cumberland's railways.

Last British Legion trip to Seascale.

Dragonfly Bridge and signal box

The Dragonfly Bridge spanned the A595 Trunk Road. The road was closed on 27th June 1957 for improvements. The road level was reduced by 4 feet, giving a bridge height clearance of 16 feet 6 inches. Double-decker buses could only pass through in the middle of the road before this. On the weekend of 23rd and 24th June 1979, the bridge was demolished. The Highways Agency of the Cumberland County Council, decided that the expense of maintaining the bridge was becoming too much, so they ordered the removal of the bridge. The road was closed to all traffic at 11.00pm on Saturday 23rd June 1979. A large amount of soil was tipped under the bridge to protect the road surface and the gas main from being damaged. At 7.00am the following morning, the demolition charges were detonated by the daughter of the C.C.C. Bridge Engineer, 16 year old Lesley Mole of Scotby, Carlisle. A large crowd witnessed the explosion. A nearby bungalow, Barffs Sykes, owned by Cyril Dalton, had been boarded up but still had some broken windows. Glaziers on standby carried out all repairs very quickly. Mr and Mrs Dalton and their son had sheltered in their garage workshops during the explosion. The road reopened on the following Tuesday morning. Soon after, the bridge over the road at the top of Swallow Hill was also demolished the same way over a weekend.

After demolition

INNS and TAVERNS

Distington had its own Brewery in 1749. It was set up by William Birkett and Son, the proprietors of the Castle Inn pub on the main road at the junction with Swallow Hill. The Brewery was at the bottom of Boot Brow, on the south side of the beck and on the left hand side when travelling towards Whitehaven. They set up a bottling plant on the upper floor of the Castle pub. By 30th October 1883, the brewery had been taken over by Joseph Dalziel of Parton Brewery. At this time, the Castle 'beer house' was occupied by Elizabeth Simpson.

There were a number of pubs in the village going back through the centuries. Pubs from 1393 had to have a 'Picture' sign over their front door, under a law by Richard II and many of these signs still survive. This was to make pubs recognisable to the public, who could not read. Eight public houses and two clubs have been listed in the village. Inns and taverns listed in an 1847 Mannix and Whellan directory were:

Queens Head Hotel -
landlady Mrs Eliza Henderson,

Black Lion Inn –
landlord James Lightfoot,

Globe Hotel –
landlord Robert Bell,

Hope Inn –
landlord James Newton,

Black Cock Inn –
landlady Mrs Sarah Kitchen,

Robin Hood Inn –
landlord John White, (he was also limestone cutter at Barngill Gate).

The Hare and Hounds, Pica, which later became the Greyhound Inn,

Thomas Smith of the Castle Inn was not on this list as it was only an Ale-house.

The first club was the Coronation Club and took over the former stables building to the rear of the Globe Inn. It was set up between the two world wars and was better known as the British Legion. The Legion moved to Church Road when they bought the Mission Chapel Hall and opened the new club in 1937. The Legion still has the name Coronation Club in its title. Distington men Jimmy Comrie and Cyril Hodgson were both club secretaries in their time. Cyril Hodgson received the OBE for his long service of 50 years in the Legion.

In May 1986, the Rugby Club was built alongside the playing pitch beside Hinnings Road and it supported the sports ground. Only the Castle and the Globe still operate as pubs. The Queens Head was known as the Kings Head until Queen Victoria came to the throne in 1837.

In the past, the pub has played a major part in the activities in Distington. A sheriff, who was appointed by the village squire to keep law and order, operated from the upper floor of the pub. Stairs were built to the upper floor at the rear of the pub. It was totally separate from the ground floor. The sheriff was able to recruit up to ten men as a posse when required. The village stocks stood outside the pub. Land agents also used the upstairs level of the pub. Daily deliveries of mail from Whitehaven came by stagecoach in the days before the Post Office was built, and Edward Dryden used the office in his duties as Registrar. The pub ceased to operate as a pub in the summer of 2000. It became the Jade Palace, a Chinese takeaway and is now known as the Taste of China.

The Black Lion, a Matthew Brown pub, is now a private residence, 71 Main Street and records date this back to 1645. The iron spiral staircase, outside the front of the building and leading to the upper floor, was taken down in 1948. The pub closed in 1974.

Queens Head

Black Lion

Boot Inn

Black Cock Inn

The Castle

Grey Hound

The Globe

Sign above the door of The Globe

The Globe Hotel, which was a Lion Brewery pub and became a free house in its later years, is on the site of a very old building. A date of 1477 was marked on the doorway of the market garden adjacent to the pub in the Middle-Ages and is one of only a few public houses still to have a picture sign hanging on the front wall. There is ground behind the recently renovated wall. In the days of the stagecoach, horses were kept in stables at the rear of the pub and passengers could stop overnight. A regular service ran from Whitehaven to Carlisle and Kendal, passing through each morning except Sundays, calling in at the Globe to change horses. A passageway next to the pub carried a painted notice saying, 'Post horses only'. The painted sign faded but remained until the house next door, number 80, was knocked down in January, 1976. The Globe ceased trading in early 2007 for a short period but is trading again now.

The Antelope is now a hairdressing salon. Previously, this pub was known as the Hope and Anchor, well known it its time when run by Mrs Ada Bowman. Ada Bowman was also the manageress of the Enterprise Cinema, which was part of the Myers and Bowman's complex. There is more of Myers and Bowman's in another chapter.

The Black Cock stood at the beginning of the road to Beck Green. This pub also sold Matthew Brown's ales, and was closed down in 1974. After the Second World War, Mrs Harriet Beatty, later Mrs Foy, made the pub popular because of her interest in Hound Trails. The house to the right of the pub, No 5 Beck Green, was leased out by the brewery. Mr and Mrs Messenger and their family lived there for many years before moving to 6 Gilgarran View. Another family followed, Bob and Isabel Paterson, who leased No 5 from brewery manager Harold Eastwood, and lived there with their disabled son Philip. The door into number five was moved from the centre of the front of this house between two windows to the left to its present position, in place of one of the windows. When removing an old wall covering, a flight of stairs was found leading to an attic. Philip had built a large model train set and

spent many hours up there. A residence for elderly people was built by Harriet's son, Tony Foy and is adjacent to Distington Park. This was named after Harriet. She died on 16th December 1984, aged 92.

The Boot, now known as Boot House, was at the bottom of the hill at Common End and closed down about 1986. It was originally built for the dray horses belonging to the William Birkett brewery.

Next in line was the Castle Inn, on the main road at the Common End junction with Swallow Hill. It was opened in 1749. In the 1881 census, it was recorded as an alehouse, not a pub, because it sold beer only. The building did not get a spirits licence until 1958. The Castle brewed its own beer, as reported at the beginning of this chapter. A bottling plant was in the upper floor of the building and later at the rear of the pub for many years. Until 1958, The Castle public house was a free house. The original pub was split into three small rooms. The house below the pub was bought and opened up as an extra bar. The dividing walls were removed to make the pub as it is today. It became part of the Scottish and Newcastle Group. Today, it is a free house again. A story says that there was a secret passage to Hayes Castle from here. If this is so then it may have been to an older pub on the same site.

On 18th April 1987, an Easter weekend, a woman was shot and killed on the doorstep of the Castle Inn pub when Tommy and Jean Graham ran the pub.

The Robin Hood was at the boundary of the parish at Barngill. Before modern transport, farmers had to walk their livestock to the Whitehaven Auction Market. The pub was a handy place for the farmers to stop overnight. The cattle and sheep were kept in the field opposite, now owned by Hayescastle Farm and is the site of the Annual Vintage Rally, held to show steam rollers, old cars, motorcycles and machinery.

At Studfold, Pica, on the road to Dean stood the Greyhound public house. It was originally called the Hare and Hounds pub. This was the home of Billy Myers and Ada Bowman's parents when Billy Myers joined forces with Bill Bowman to repair cycles and farm machinery. When work increased, they rented a farm byre at the southern end of the Main Street, Distington, where Rathbones now stands, and developed into the biggest motor engineering works in the North of England.

SCHOOLS

Dame schools were operating in the village during the 18th century. These were usually in one room of a private house on the Main Street. Those who could afford the fees sent their children to be taught how to read and write. Dame schools were in use in Distington and in Gilgarran Hamlet. There was also a school in Barngill.

The first recognised school under the then new Education Act of 1750 was at Common End and is now a private home. Funding was raised by people of the village. The master, James Woodall, was given the rights of tithes in 1770 on three acres of common land as his sole income, giving him an income of about £20 per year. Attendance of pupils was on a voluntary basis.

Described in its day as a very fine building, a new school was built on Main Street. It was built in red sandstone, dug from local quarries at Pica, cost £3,000 and was opened on 2nd January 1877. It had accommodation for 280 children. On the first day, there were no desks or books. It reopened on 8th January with 53 pupils. In 1886, Dyon School Pica was opened. Windscales School, where the BP petrol station is now, opened in 1891. Children from the Furnace Row area were transferred there. All fees were dropped when the Education Act of 1891 gave free education to all pupils

A school board committee was set up. John Robertson-Walker became chairman and Edward Dryden, village registrar, was the clerk of the committee. Other members were Hugh Munro McKenzie of Prospect House, John Studholme, master mariner, Joseph Harrison, coal dealer of Town Head, Thomas Garrett, yeoman farmer, Will Yates, tailor, John Richardson of Croft Cottage, Reverend W W Wodehouse, Rector, John Salkeld of Hinnings farm, Henry Southward, miller of Millyard, Town Head, John Bewley and John Poole. The first school headmaster was James Bryning and

the first headmistress was Miss M Bryning. Later school board members included Dr Henry Castles, Reverend N Hodgson and the Reverend T Fellowes, curate at the church.

In 1902, the Secondary School became only the second school in the county to have a clock tower. The clock was started by Miss Angela Hodgson, the daughter of the Rector, the Rev W. W. Hodgson. The school closed for one week for the coronation of King Edward VII. The population of the three schools was approximately 500.

Around this time, Sarah Kirkpatrick started work as a teacher. She worked unpaid for 12 months before passing an exam and was then paid 1 shilling (5p) per week. She said she was always late after working on the farm on Main Street and could be seen running down the road in her clogs. Sarah lived all her life in Distington and died when in her nineties.

Distington claimed a first when the County Minor Award was given to May Kendall, aged 11. In 1911, the school closed for one week for the Coronation of George V. It also closed for one day when Miss Diane Robertson-Walker got married. Could such a thing happen today?

Other days off were for King's and Queen's birthdays, Orange Day parades, church choir picnics and a visit to Distington Hall. There was also Mr Birkett's sports day at Common End and for a visit to Distington by Barnum and Bailey's circus.

In 1912, the school got a garden. Competitions were set among the pupils to improve their gardening skills and a cup was awarded to the best pupils. Charlie Wilkinson of Kilnside won the first cup followed by his brother Stan soon after. In 1913, six trees were planted in front of the school.

In 1924, Windscales School closed down and

became a bed and breakfast hotel. Myers and Bowman's new bus, the Lady Florence, driven by Billy Myers then bussed in the pupils to Distington.

School milk started in 1934; it cost ½pence per bottle. In January, 1936, the school closed for the funeral of King George V. At the same time, electric lighting was installed. When war was declared on 3rd September 1939, the school closed again but re-opened five days later with 62 evacuees plus three teachers from Newcastle. From August, 1944, evacuees from London also came here for three years. At the end of the war, Queen Elizabeth, later the Queen Mother, sent a certificate of thanks to all people who took in the schoolchildren and looked after them so well when most had never been away from home before.

A stirrup pump was sent to the school to teach the children what to do when a bomb hit the school. Money was collected for the war effort and by March 1943, the school had saved £2,900. The following year, the infants were asked to collect £100. They collected £462. At the end of the war, two days of holiday celebrated VE Day and VJ Day, victory in Europe 8th May 1945 and victory over Japan 15th August 1945. Two rooms in the Sunday

School were used after WW II as extra classrooms for the nine and ten year old children.

The Victoria Hall and later the Coronation Hall were used for school mid-day lunches. In 1948 and 1949, three concrete prefabricated buildings were erected. One was for two extra classrooms. The second was for woodwork classes for the boys and domestic science classes for the girls, with pupils from Parton, Lowca and Moresby visiting in their turn. Prior to this Distington children had to travel by bus, to Harrington Junior school, now Beckstone Bridge Primary school, at the top of the hill for woodworking and domestic science lessons. The third to be built was for a canteen and kitchen. This ended the need for meals outside of the school. Miss Margaret Steel worked in the kitchens for more than 40 years. At the back of the school, a wooden hut was put up when another three classrooms were needed in 1951. In 1961, senior pupils were transferred to the new Lillyhall School, which opened at Toll-Bar. Closure of this school was first .proposed in April 1982 and this happened soon after.

Teaching staff that I remember of the Main Street School in the 1940s and 1950s was Alfred Scott, headmaster, with Chris Dixon of Millyard, Bert

Distington Secondary Modern School

Cunliffe of Bankside, Eric Thomas of Ennerdale View, Sid Hiddleston of Cleator Moor, who was a Royal Air Force bomber pilot during WW II, Jack Dunnell of Seaton, the woodwork and metalwork teacher, Mrs Polly of Whitehaven, who prepared pupils for their 11 plus examinations as did Miss Joan Tubman of Workington, Jack Byfield, Mr Colbourne of St Bees, a keen photographer, and Frank Lahiff of Frizington, a teacher who was keen on Rugby Union but had to settle for coaching Rugby League because there were not enough boys in the top class at the time. Frank later became headmaster at Frizington and died in retirement at Harrogate in 2006.

Distington Secondary Modern School became a junior school in 1961 when the Lillyhall School was built. Pupils attended Lillyhall School when they became eleven years old. In April 1982, a proposal was made to close Lillyhall School down and transfer the pupils to Southfield School, Moorclose Workington, because of falling pupil numbers. The Parish Council objected to the proposal but the change took place in September 1984.

In 1981, the clock face on the Main Street School was vandalised, putting the clock out of action. Both the Parish Council and the Education Department declined to pay for the repairs. The 135 boys and girls aged 7 to 11, decided for themselves to raise the money through sporting events. The clock was restarted in 1984. The clock again developed a fault and was converted from clockwork to be driven by an electric motor. The work was paid for by the Parish Council in 2007.

In 2002, the pupils were transferred to the new Community School after the amalgamation of the Main Street school and the Church Road school in 2001. The old school was taken over by the Social Services Department in April 2004 as an admin centre for the disabled. The Social Services Dept. had been in some months before this to create smaller individual offices in the class room areas.

The Distington Community School, was built in 1961 and stands opposite the Community Centre on Church Road. Extensions were built on to the Community School for extra classrooms, a computer room and a hall for recreation training. Further building extension work was done in 2005. The hall is used by other organisations to put on entertainment shows.

Dyon School at Pica was used for junior children up to the age of 11 and had just two classrooms. Eleven plus pupils were then transferred to Distington School, travelling in Myers and Bowman's bus. It closed down in 1969 and has been converted to become private houses.

A new college costing £11 million pounds was built on the site of Lillyhall School. The West Cumbria College, later called Lakes College West Cumbria, was built by Kier Construction and was officially opened on Tuesday 8th May 2001. The high-tech learning resource facilities centre was built to attract more students as well as a sports centre and a restaurant which could be used by outside organisations. The annual dinner for the Distington Old Folks Re-Union Club is held there every Christmas. The first principal of the college was Paul Haffren. The principal in 2008 is Kath Richardson, the same name but not the same person as the village vicar, Rev. Kath Richardson.

The prospectus for the college courses up to A level, GCSE, B TEC and HND standard in 2008 are listed as:

• Art and Design,
• Business management and I. T.,
• Childcare
• Construction
• Engineering
• Vehicle maintenance and repairs
• Public Services
• Hairdressing and Beauty Therapy
• Health and Social care
• Hospitality and Tourism
• Sports and Leisure
• Training to get an apprenticeship.

The college also gives help to attain higher education. Courses in HNC (Higher National Certificates) are held for Applied Chemistry, Electrical Engineering and Mechanical Engineering plus Operations in Plant Engineering. There is also a HNC in Business Studies, backed by the University of Central Lancashire. The University of Central Lancashire also validate a Foundation Degree in Nuclear Decommissioning. Other Foundation Degrees are in Education and care of young people, Physical Activity and Health Management with specialist pathways and Diplomas for the Chartered Accountants Institute.

DISTINGTON IRONWORKS

In 1879, The Distington Hematite Iron and Steel Company opened. Toll Bar cottages and Furness Row cottages were built for its workers. All the buildings on Furnace Row were single story buildings except No 1, which was the home of the site manager. The works had two furnaces in use, producing 600 to 700 tons of iron a week. A row of 11 boilers fed the furnaces. Ivor Harrison, a metallurgist, described the normal procedure. Hematite ore was brought into the works and crushed into a fine powder. It was then mixed with manganese, carbon, sulphur and phosphates, put into the furnaces and brought up to a temperature of up to 1500 to 1600 degrees to make pig-iron. Chromium could be added to the mixture to make wrought iron, which never rusts and was suitable

for passing on to steel works. The pig-iron was tapped into large ladles and poured into moulds to the customer's requirements. Wooden moulds were

Distington Ironworks

normally used, lying on a sand bed when making cast iron girders.

A report was published in the Mechanical and Engineering weekly journal dated 1st October 1909 of an explosion at Distington Ironworks on 18th September 1909. The explosion occurred on a Saturday afternoon at 5pm. Most of the workmen had finished at 12.30pm. Only about 30 men were still on site. The men were working behind the blast furnaces and this protected them from the blast of the explosion. The report said that the explosion was unusual in many ways when four Lancashire boilers burst at the same time. Boilers 5, 6, 7 and 8 in a line of 11 were involved. The Lancashire type boiler was 30 feet (9m) long and 8 feet (2½m) in diameter. All the boilers were connected by a common steam pipe, working at a pressure of 45 to 50lbs per square inch and were heated by the exhaust steam from the blast furnaces. Each boiler had its own set of water gauges, pressure gauges and safety valves. The boilers were well kept and in good working order. There was no warning and the blast created an enormous amount of damage. The two boilers at the centre of the explosion were unrecognisable and the others were badly damaged. Forty parts of boiler plating were found on the site and in the surrounding fields. Parts of the inner flue tubes were found on the railway line.

A boiler flew 200 yards into the air going over the tall chimney on the site and split into two pieces. The largest part must have reached a considerable height because when it landed on the road to Workington, it penetrated the road to a depth of two metres. Number eight boiler split into two halves, weighing six tons each. One part flew 400 yards towards Distington Hall. The other part landed ¼ mile away. Parts of the boiler flew over a locomotive engine standing in the loco sheds, narrowly missing the driver and fireman, who escaped with bruising from the flying bricks. The Railway Office was badly damaged. Mr Kelly, the site manager at the time, had been in there just before the explosions happened. Bricks crashed through the roof of the home of Mr Stalker of Furnace Road. The cabin of the weigh- man was

completely demolished only minutes after the man had left. Had it been in normal working hours, many people could have been hurt, but also, had men been working there, it might never have happened. Even with the large amount of damage done, not one person was seriously injured.

In most cases of boiler explosions it was easy to find the cause of the explosion but not in this case. The remaining parts were clean and no corrosion could be found. When the workers reported for work on Monday morning, the married men were kept on to clean up the site but single men were laid off. The work's clock on site did not stop.

The Ironworks Company eventually closed down in 1922. The main gates were taken to Chapel Bank Engineering Works, Workington, and can still be seen there today.

Distington Ironworks

Arrow shows the second half of boiler

POLICE IN DISTINGTON

The modern day police force first came to Whitehaven and West Cumberland in September, 1843 at the request of Lord Lonsdale. A Superintendent in charge was paid £90 per annum, his sergeant was paid £50 per annum and six constables were paid £18 per year each. From the build up of the police service following this, villages throughout the area gradually got their own stations.

A Police Station in Distington came as the force expanded. In the 1881 census, the village policeman was listed as Constable William Gilbertson of Town Head, now known as Mill-Yard. In 1894, the Constable occupying the Police Station was William Wilkinson and by 1901, Thomas Bowman had taken over. 64 Main Street became the police house before moving to 5 Commonside in the mid 1930s. This was the home of Police Constable Jim Lowther, who lived there after WW II. He was awarded the Police Medal for bravery for arresting an armed murderer at Oxenholme. Another Distington man, David Tinnion was also involved in this action when in the police force. After many years in Distington, Jim Lowther was posted to Whitehaven and promoted to the rank of sergeant.

Another officer, who lived in Ennerdale View, was P C Ramsey Moore. He was on traffic duties and could be seen riding around on a Triumph Speed Twin 500 cc motor-cycle. Village police at this time included P C Charles Tappin, who also had two years in service in Cyprus. Others to come later were Jack Holmes, Dougie Cook, George Moffatt, Peter Thorp and Peter Franklin, later to become a sergeant. He was the last to live in the police house. Special Constable Moore lived on Barffs Road and Jack Holmes lived in Distington Park after his retirement. He died in 1994. Designated policeman for the village in 2004 was P C Brockbanks. He attended duties in the village when required. A new police house was built at Millyard in 1954 and was sold in 1994 as a private house when community policing replaced the man on the beat.

A Distington schoolboy, John Garner from 2 Gilgarran View, joined the Workington Police Force straight from school, aged 16. He served three years as a cadet before becoming a fully trained police officer. He rose through the ranks, serving many places in Cumbria, including Workington, Carlisle and Kendal. He worked in both the uniformed branch and the C I D before becoming a Superintendent, taking charge of the West Cumbria area. He retired in July 2007 after 30 years service.

THE VILLAGE IN THE 20TH CENTURY

In the local Government Act of 1894, Ennerdale Rural District Council was formed. At the same time, the Distington Parish Council was begun. The chairman of Ennerdale RDC from its beginning was the Reverend William George Courtenay Hodgson, MA, JP, CC, a post he held for 20 years until his death in 1914. Other RDC members from Distington included Mr Charles Fisher, JP, of Distington Hall, Thomas Dobie, ironmonger, William Turner, stationmaster, William Harrison, farmer, Thomas Wilson, architect, George Elliot, miner, Joseph Falcon, schoolmaster, Jacob Timmins, ironworker and John Seeds, railway signalman. The Ennerdale RDC ended on 1st April 1974 when Copeland Council was formed and Distington Parish Council continued as before.

In 1901, members of the Parish Council were Charles Fisher, of Distington Hall, J Robertson-Walker, Edward Harrison, Joseph Robinson, John Seeds, John Roper, J Timmins, Lance Salkeld, John Bewley, A Harris, Thomas Smith, Edward Plaskett, George Elliot and Tom Wilson. John Salkeld was clerk to the council. Rev. W Hodgson and Lance Salkeld were also District Councillors.

The School Board consisted of Rev. W Hodgson, Dr Henry Castles, MD, John Roper, Edward Plaskett and W Wilson. The clerk was W Birkett.

The Parish Council in March, 2004 had John Bowman as chairman with Reg Gallagher as vice chairman. The other councillors were Mrs Jackie Bowman, Miss M Bramly, Mary Canfield, Victoria Gee, Barry Kirkwood, David Richardson, Robin and Kath Sharpe, Roy Shepherd, Joe Stephenson, Betty Walker and Henry Ward. Councillor Cam Ross is also on the Cumbria County Council. Brian Dixon, Mrs Willis Metherel and Kevin Young are also on Copeland Council. Willis Metherell became Mayor of Copeland in 2006. The Parish had a population of 3,431 in 1991 and increased to 3,944 in the census of 2001. Distington is the largest village in this area of West Cumbria. Many houses date back over a long time. A house opposite the Reading Room has a date of 1724 carved into the lintel above the front door.

In 1906, Jennings Brother's vehicles, powered by motor-engines were reported as causing damage to the road surface due to their heavy weight, leaving deep ruts in the un-surfaced road, which was a problem to pedestrians and cattle. In 1912, the number of fatal accidents on Main Street worried the council of that time, so they asked the police to enforce a speed limit of 8 mph. The signs for the present speed limit area remain the same place today at Toll Bar and Common End.

The by-pass, built from Millyard to near Beck Green, was opened in 1935. This relieved the village of all the through traffic. The steep hill on this road was reduced in 1964 and 1965 when the high point was lowered by 19 feet and was also re-aligned at the same time. The slope on the road from the Cenotaph to the Boot was altered at the same time. A new by-pass is now being built and is due to open in December 2008.

The village had a surgery in 1880. The doctor was Dr Henry Castles, a Whitehaven surgeon who lived in Town Head. A new surgery was built when Attorgarth House was erected in 1903. In the 1930s, the husband and wife team, the doctors, Mr and Mrs Watson, with Mrs Watson's brother, Doctor Hugh Calder, a surgeon, provided a service for the village. They had two rooms of their house for patients to attend, just turning up on the day, no appointment needed. They also took on the system of dispensing their own drugs which is still continuing today in the modern surgery.

In 1963, Dr James Sharp took a risk when building a new surgery at Hinnings Road. The National

May Festival Dancing 1915.

Health Service did not fund the work so he built it in the shape of a bungalow. A number of improvements have taken place since then. Into the 21st century, it now has a staff of four permanent doctors, Dr Bater, Dr Rudman, Dr Booth and Dr Naylor. Two other doctors are on six month contracts. There are three nurses and three district nurses and a dispensary. With receptionists, the number on the staff is up to 19.

Two men from the parish left here to make their name in America. An item in the church magazine of 1928 reported that Mr Bobbie Harding started working at Oatlands Colliery Pica when he was thirteen years old. When he emigrated to America, he continued in mining and prospecting until he became a mine owner. He became controller of mining interests in both America and Canada. For many years he was an official of the American Miners Federation and edited a miner's magazine. In 1919, he attended the Versailles Conference to represent the interests of the Labour Party. He was president of the Seattle City Council for many years until in 1931 he was elected the city's first Labour Mayor of Seattle.

Mr Norman Tolson was the second man who emigrated to America. He distinguished himself when studying at the Kansas City School of Fine Art and the Chicago Art Institute, also in Munich and Kensington. He returned to America in 1914 and concentrated on commercial art for six years. He took up teaching at Kansas and later at Balliol College, Wisconsin. Later still, he moved to Milwaukee. A glance in America's 'Who's Who in American Art' shows Mr Tolson to be the recipient of many honours and awards in many branches of art.

A newspaper reported in 1934 that Barngill House, on the boundary of the parish was once the home of Britain's richest man. He was Sir John Ellerman. In a record of Britain's millionaires, he came top of the list with the next man earning less than half his earnings. He started in banking and formed a shipping company, Ellerman Lines Shipping Company, whose ships operated all over the world. He became a recluse and avoided the limelight that his fame later brought him. He died in 1933. In a tax report in the 1920s, it was said that he had nearly 500 million pounds to his name.

A certificate of the wedding of Lawrence Wilkinson's parents, dated February 1930 said that Kilnside from its junction with Church Road to the flat top houses was then called Quarry Road.

In 1921, a complaint was put to the council about

A typical family of the 1920s. L to R: Joe, Daisy, Ruth, Grandma, George, Granda, Angela & Stephen.
The Wilkinson Family of 15 Church Road. Circa 1925.

the lack of building new houses in the village. However, only 24 houses were built between the two world wars. During the 2nd World War, housing was required for the people working at the new High Duty Alloys factory, known throughout Distington as HDA. This is when the flat top houses of the Barffs Road Estate were built, starting with Barffs Road in 1942. Other roads were Kilnside Road, Kilnside Place, Glebe Road, Rectory Place, Rectory Square, Bankside and finishing at Gilgarran View in 1943. My parents moved into Gilgarran View in August, 1943, when my dad was working in the foundry of the HDA. Before this, we had lived in Hensingham and dad had to cycle to and from work whatever the weather.

At the turn of the 21st century, many of these houses had become worse for wear, and were being knocked down in June, 2001. In the 1950s, the Hinnings Road estate was built, housing many people from Parton. These two estates greatly increased the population of the village. Altogether, about 250 houses were built.

Prominent people and business men and women listed in the 1901 version of Bulmer's Directory

Distington Main Street (sketch by Ben Cope)
Courtesy of Whitehaven News

were listed as follows. The Rector, Rev W W Hodgson, village registrar Edward Dryden, Doctor Henry Castles, MD, Joshua Brunskill, school master who lived in the house next door to the school, No 64, which has been occupied by Cissie Tinnion for over fifty years and Daniel Carver of Barngill school. John Moncur, Distington Ironworks manager also lived on Main Street, The station master was William Campbell and the

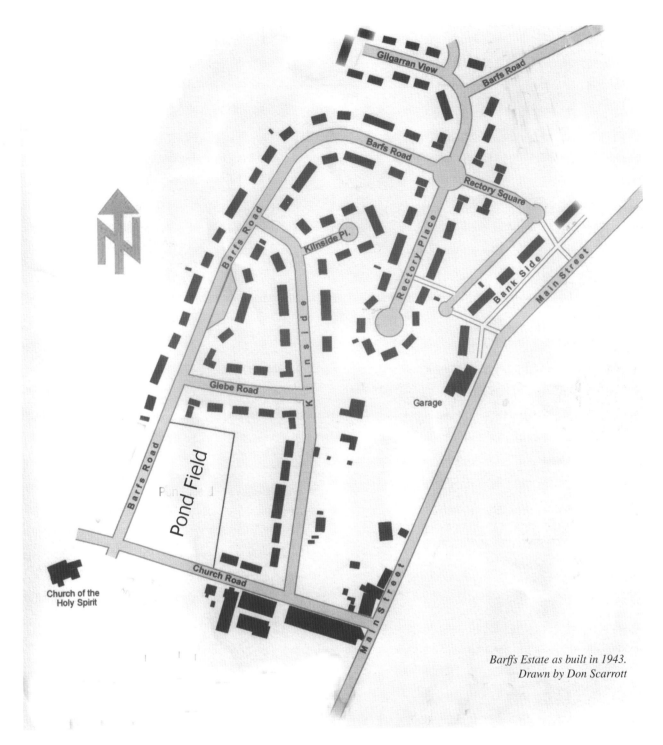

Church of the
Holy Spirit

Pond Field

Garage

Barffs Estate as built in 1943.
Drawn by Don Scarrott

railways agent was John Kelly. A master mariner John Studholme was well known in the village. Shop keepers listed were seed merchant John Bewley, two cycle agents John Crookdake and Christopher Clark, who also ran the Post Office, postman William Fearon, John Chalmers, butcher, two tailors, Wilson Tolson of Boot brow and Henry Kirkpatrick and pub landlords, William Crone of Robin Hood, Mary Frears, Globe, Annie Irwin, Hope and Anchor and I Pollock, Boot.

Tradesmen listed included three blacksmiths.

They were Jonathon Crookdake, Joseph Tolson and Mathew Bewley. Jonathon Crookdake's forge was at Pandora Terrace and is referred to in a later chapter. Joseph Tolson and Mathew Bewley both had a forge on Main Street. A forge was in the present No 81 Main Street, now the home of Jim Stevenson. It was the forge of Mathew Bewley. Remains of the forge were found during alterations when modernising the house. Wheat chaff was also found under the floorboards on the upper floor, which would have been the store room. At each side were a stable and a workroom. The date 1706 is

39

above the door. The other forge was in the barn of Ulpha Glebe farm. The building is opposite number 100B Main Street. The double doors are still there today and the building is used as a garage and workshop.

There were two catering rooms run by Mrs Matilda Nevin and Dinah Owen. The two joiners were Lancelot Salkeld and William Gregson. The boot and shoe maker was D C Hepburn and a cab proprietor Mrs J Kirkpatrick lived in Midtown House. Robert Shaw was also listed as living in Toll Bar Cottage.

In Distington, the Co-operative store was the Workington District Co-operative and the one in Pica was the Cleator Moor Co-operative Society. These shops are usually referred to as the Co-op.

The Distington Reading Room secretary was William Turner.

In Pica, there were Tom and William Beatie, caterers, Tom Baydon, 63 Pica Cottages, Cleator Moor Co-operative manager Joseph Percival, J Giddens, Dyonside, schoolmaster, George Miller, Oatlands Pit surface manager, Moresby Coal Co. manager Archibald Thom and John Myers, Greyhound Public House victualer. The Pica Reading Room secretary was John Roper.

In Gilgarran, there were James Bruce, estate gamekeeper, and James Eland, Hill House, Gilgarran,

Farmers in the Parish were Robinson Burns of Whin Bank, Henry Chapman Summer View, Christopher and James Clark Kelmore Hill, John Cowan Dyonside, John Dickenson of Woolcroft, who was also a game keeper, John Fawkes, Lodge Castle Farm, .William Gregain, Spring Hill, Tom Graham, Wilson Park, John Harrison, Town End Farm, William Harrison, Hayes Castle, John Holiday, Colingate, George Jackson, Midtown Farm, Daniel Lightfoot, Hinnings, William Marshall, Town End, David Messenger, Dyonside and of Hill House, Peter Robinson, Oatlands Farm, Tom Salkeld, Beckside, Francis Sewell, Fairfield, Tom Smith, Stubsgill, William Southward, Boonwood, Martha Stewart, Barffs Syke, William Stewart, Dyon Hill and William Thompson of The Green. Geordie Clark ran a coach drawn by four horses from Distington to Whitehaven for two years before motor buses started in 1920. Robinson Burns did

the same from Pica.

When men returned from the First World War, there was no work for many of them. It was usual for men to congregate on a daily basis at the Queens Head corner or at the Lodge on the drive to Prospect House. The lodge is opposite the Antelope. Their children ran about the street in bare feet.

Distington has an organisation called the Distington Old Folks Re-union Club, set up to help the over 65s living in the Distington Parish area. The club was started before the First World War in 1912. Margaret Steele remembers that John Casson, Mr Wilson and George Wilkinson were committee members, among others, for many years during the 1930s. In the years after the Second World War, Harry Kitchen, Albert Wilkinson, Jim Murray, Robert Henry Taylor, James and Henry Allen, Mr Douglas, who was landlord of the Queens Head pub, Tom Williamson, Tom McCracken, Robert Graham, Bert Stewart, Bob Wilson, William Crossfield, James Steele, George Todhunter, John Bird, Thomas Bateman, Colin Crossfield, James Gregson and Jack Holmes all had a role in the organisation. Others who took part in the more recent years were Peter Canfield, Alec Graham, Joe Maughan, Robin Sharpe and Tommy Graham. Dr Sharpe was President for many years. There was a Ladies Committee comprising of Margaret Steele, Kathleen McSherry, Isobel Riddick, Molly Smallwood, Lizzie Gregson, Lizzie Wilson, Elsie Graham, Mrs Banks. Mrs Allan and Enid Poole who all served to help out with the meals etc.

Money was raised by holding concerts in the Victoria Hall and also by whist drives. They also held raffles with tickets priced at one shilling, that's five pence in today's money. Margaret Steele's brother, Tommy, born in 1920, remembers singing in concerts during the 1920s. John W. Mitchell, headmaster of Distington School, was auditor of the annual accounts on a regular basis. At the Christmas re-union, he was always the man who stood up and proposed a vote of thanks for the committee's work. He never missed an outing until he was in his late eighties.

The re-union meal was first held in the Sunday School room on Church Road. The ladies who attended were given a gift of a tea caddy and the men were given tobacco. This used to be held on New Years Day.

Silloth Outing 1936. Men in the above photograph are Jim Murray, a committee member, John Casson, Bill Smith, William Birkett of the Castle Inn, Jim Allan, also on the committee, J Nicholson, Mr Nicholson of Sunny Brow, John Salkeld, Curly Douglas, Jonathon Dryden, Stephen Scott, Richard John Hall, Bateman Murray and Robert Henry. He was known throughout the area as Pem.

The club started organising outings. In 1936, a trip was arranged to visit Silloth. It is not known if there were any outings before this. After WW II, Ray Studholme, known throughout the village as Studs, and his wife Betty, both served on the committee at one time. They joined up with Bert Stewart and hired a bus from Kirkpatrick's to go to Workington to collect the food needed for the annual dinner. It was prepared and cooked at Distington School.

The Club is still active today. On 14th July 2007, four coaches took 160 people out for the day. First stop was to the Shepherds Inn in Carlisle for a meal and then we were taken to Bowness-on-Windermere for a few hours before returning home after having an enjoyable time. In 2004, the club took us to Shap Wells Hotel for a three course meal and then on to Lancaster. The following year, we went to the fore-mentioned Shepherds Inn and then on to Dumfries. A Christmas dinner and entertainment takes place each December. In 2006, there were 200 guests sitting for dinner at the Lakes College. Coaches were arranged to take people from the village to

the college and returned back to the village at the end of the outing. All this is free for the over 65s. The committee still collect money by holding three sweeps per year and also having Bingo nights every Monday evening.

The President now is Ron Shillito, who took over when Dr Burgess retired. Dr Burgess had taken over when Dr Sharpe died in 1993. Colin McBride is the chairman and has been for 25 years. The secretary is Mike Tierney and the treasurer is John Cowen. The present committee is W Weightman, M Stewart, R Speight, B McSherry, D Armstrong, B Jenkinson, K Mason and P Gilmore. The ladies helping out today are Margaret McBride, Phyllis Cowan, Lorraine Gilmore, Jane Mason, Susan Stewart, Kath Winstanley, Sandra Armstrong and Joan Jenkinson. Long may this proud tradition continue.

A War Memorial was erected in a field adjacent to the main road to Whitehaven, opposite Beck Green. It was unveiled and dedicated on the 16th April, 1921. A local architect, Thomas Wilson of Flower

A Ladies Committee, circa 1970. Back Row, L to R: Maggie Allen, Lizzie Wilson, Enid Poole, Molly Smallwood & Elsie Graham. Front Row, L to R: Margaret Steele, Lizzie Gregson & Ginny Banks.

Remembrance Sunday

Some of those in the march can be seen in the above photograph. In the front row are John Boyd. Jack Holmes and Bob McCracken. On the left behind Jack is Cyril Hodgson and in the centre is Joe Jolly. In the light raincoat is Bert Stewart. The last four on the right are George Cole, Ron Shillito, Ray Studholme and Bob Spedding. This photo was taken circa 1970.

Hill, arranged for the building of the monument. The Memorial was transferred to the Parish Council with an agreement that the Council would take care of the maintenance of the monument in January, 1923. A service and a march to the Memorial takes place every year on the Sunday nearest to Armistice Day, 11th hour of the 11th day of the 11th month, 1918, when peace was declared at the end of the WW I. The then Prince of Wales, who became King Edward VIII and later became the Duke of Windsor after his abdication, visited the monument during his tour of distressed areas in June, 1927.

An unemployment club was opened at 58 Main Street, now demolished, between the Post Office and the Chapel. This later became the Old Age Pensioners club and was visited by the Duke of Kent in 1936. The club was known as the 'Pig and Whistle'. The Duke then visited the Miners Welfare in Pica. The Duke was killed in action during the Second World War.

Mains electricity came to the village in 1934/35. The supply was originally on wooden poles running the length of the Main Street carrying 240 volts AC single phase and 415 volt three phase supplies. After a number of power-cuts due to storm damage, these poles were removed and replaced with underground cables early into the 21st century.

Street lighting first came after an Act of Parliament in 1620 ordered people to have a burning torch hanging beside their front door. When local councils were formed, it became their responsibility. Oil burning lamps were first used by the Parish Council. After the WW II, street lighting lanterns were fitted to the Electricity Board's wooden poles, each with a 100 watt lamp. These were controlled from two time-switches, one at the southern steps to Bankside and the other at the Lodge, opposite the Antelope. The same system applied to Common End. A time-switch on a pole near to Museum Villas, still there, controlled Boot Brow and Swallow Hill. During the lighting improvements of the 1950s, the trunk road columns were fitted with the modern 135 watt sodium lighting. The 100 watt lamps, with a life expectancy of 6 weeks have been replaced with 70 watt sodium lamps with a four year lifespan.

In the 1931 census, Distington had a population of 1,821. In 1938, just before the Second World War, many businesses names were handed down from father to son. These businesses were listed in Kelly's Directory as follows:

- Sarah Armstrong, shopkeeper, Main Street,
- Thomas Arnison, builder, Common End,
- James Batt, registrar, Albert Hall,
- Hannah Bennett, sweet shop, Millyard,
- George Lamby Branthwaite, hairdresser, Main Street,
- William Campbell, coal agent, Distington Station,
- Charles Clark, Post Office and grocers,
- John Crookdake and Sons, motor engineers and smithy,
- Myers and Bowman, engineering works and dance hall,
- Gilf Dixon, fruiterer, Main Street,
- Edward Fox, grocers, Wellington House,
- Alfred Green, builder, Town Head,
- Samuel Johnson, market gardener, Main Street, (adjacent to Globe Hotel),
- Midland Bank, Main Street
- Mary Murray, shopkeeper, Main Street.

The Cleator Moor Cooperative shops were both busy shops in Distington and Pica.

In Pica, there were Sarah Anderson, shopkeeper, Ben Bawden, shopkeeper, Joseph Blenkinsopp, Post Office and grocer and Henrietta Mossop, shopkeeper. Richard Hunter was a Turf Accountant in Pica.

The Secretary of Distington Reading Room was Ben Hodgson while the Secretary of Pica Reading Room was William Dryden. The proprietor of the Victoria Hall was William Douglas, who was also the landlord of the Queens Head pub. At the Albert Hall, Henry Sewell was the Receiving Officer. Lance Salkeld was a joiner at Town Head, William Russell ran the newsagent's. Tom Wilson was a grocer on the Main Street and William Wilson was a grocer on Chapel Street. At Common End, George Tolson was a dentist and Doctors George Watson and his wife Margaret were in 'Attorgarth'

Pub landlords and landladies were :

- Black Lion - William Messenger,
- Black Cock - Harriet Beatie,
- Globe - Annie Lawson,
- Hope and Anchor- Ernest Bowman,
- Boot Inn - Ron Clark,
- Castle Inn - James Birkett

All these pubs were in Distington. Near to Pica was the Greyhound Inn, whose landlord was Reg Hancock.

Farmers in the Parish were:

- Jim Arnott, of Wilson Park
- William Barnes, Kenmore Hill
- Jim Brayton, Hayes Castle farm
- George Briggs, Beckside
- Jimmy Clark, Distington Hall farm
- Nathan Coates, Middle Ghyll
- William Crone, Whin Bank
- John Davy, Hinnings
- John Dickenson, Westcroft
- George Gate, Stubsgill
- Joseph Gate, Fairfield
- John Graham, Dyonside
- Gilf Gregain, Spring Hill
- James McSherry, Midtown farm (opposite Hinnings Road)
- Herbert Taylor, also Midtown farm in the centre of the village
- David Messenger, High House farm
- John Messenger, Home Farm, Gilgarran
- James Mitchinson, Oatlands
- William Southward, Boonwood
- Emmanuel Stalker, Commonside
- John Todhunter, Low Dyonside
- James Tyson, also Low Dyonside
- Walter Tinnion, Lodge Castle
- Mark Watson, Dyon Hall

James Pattinson had a smallholding at Prospect Farm, as did Mary Murray. Albert Dixon was a market gardener at Springfield. Jessie Harrison had a smallholding at Town Head and Sam Johnson was also a market gardener.

After WW II, there were still many businesses in the village. Starting from the northern end of the village, Benny Hodgson ran a sweet shop from No 1 Toll Bar Cottages. Dr Grant had a surgery at number one Furnace Row, the only two storey house on the row. It had been the furnace manager's house when the row of cottages was built for the Ironworks Company. Mr and Mrs Banks had a greengrocer's shop on Furnace Row. There was also a chip shop here. Albert Cowan sold Sunday newspapers and lived in The Lodge at the bottom of Furnace Row. His main point for selling was adjacent to number one Toll Bar Cottages. Queues used to form here for over an hour. He later moved to 6 Rectory Square.

Below Tollbar, at Barffs Syke Garage, a motor repair business was run by Cyril Dalton. At the bottom of the hill opposite Millyard, Ernie Lamb at Town Head farm had a coal yard where he delivered to the village. Ernie used his lorry to help many people moving furniture or collecting trees for goal posts for the football and rugby teams, for example. He set up his business in 1944. At eight Millyard Cottages, Harriet Bennett had a sweet shop.

Opposite Pandora Terrace was Distington Motors run by John Briggs and Russell Grant. This was closed down on 9th July 2005. This was the garage of J S Crookdake and Sons. Adjacent to 29 Pandora Terrace, the Crookdake family ran a blacksmith's forge for over 100 years. When the forge was in use, there was a room above the smithy. John Lace used this room when he set up business as a joiner and undertaker. When Lance Salkeld retired, John Lace leased the barn at Town Head to continue his trade.

Adjacent to Distington Motors garage, is a green hut which sells newspapers and sweets. This had been owned in 1951 by W E Russell and was followed by Mr Wilson. It was then run by Rodney Simpson until the end of December 2007 when Eric Skillen took over.

At Mid Town Farm, Ronnie Taylor ran a fruit and vegetable business from 1951 to 1955, selling in the village from a horse and cart. His sister Jean helped out by selling to people who came to the door. Ronnie took over the business from his dad. Another farm was also called Mid Town Farm. This stood further down the Main Street where Distington Park is now and was owned by the McSherry family. Both farms had at one time been owned by the Robertson-Walker Estate and may have been one business in their time.

Garret's Row was a row of terraced cottages to the right of the Victoria Hall. There was a Ladies hairdresser, 'Chez Ann' in the middle of the row. Next to the Victoria Hall was a small hut with a corrugated tin roof. This was the fish and chip shop of Annie Hodgson and it later became Donaldson's butcher shop.

Cleator Moor Co-operative Society, once Workington District Co-operative in 1900, is the biggest shop in the centre of the village at No 53, opposite Church Road. It was split into two parts, the groceries section and the clothing dept. The manager was Brian Benson, a well-known local councillor and at one time was the mayor of the borough. The shop re-opened on Tuesday, 10th July 2001 as a Superstore. £200,000 was spent on making improvements.

In the 1950s, Annie Hodgson moved her chip shop over the road into two house's in a row of five cottages opposite Church Road. A slaughter house stood behind these cottages when a butcher's shop was there. On the opposite corner at number 32 was J. J. Lowes Stores, a greengrocer's shop which stood at the junction with Church Road. Before this, the shop was owned by J Southward. The shop was then owned by Bill Foster and is now run by his son Lloyd, fitting car radios and repairing television sets.

Continuing down the Main Street, Bella (Cabbie) Wrangham had a sweet shop at No 67. Opposite was Lynda Elliot's hairdressing salon at No 40. Lynda also runs a mobile hairdressing business. The Midland Bank had an office at 77, next to the Black Lion public house and opposite was a betting shop at No 50. These two places are now private houses. The Post Office has been at No 54 since moving from the upper floor of the Queens Head pub many years ago. Mr Clarke, Drew Wilson, Donald Hunter and Jim and Sandra Lewthwaite have been postmasters. In 1951 the telephone number was 230. Stan Grant's bakery shop was in the block of 97, 99 and 101. Stan advertised his shop as number 97. Stan's business was S & M Grant and advertised his shop as 'TAKE IT FOR GRANTed.' It closed down in 1999 when a serious defect in the old wall above the doorway of the shop meant that the shop was condemned and had to be demolished.

Stan's sons told me that he had learnt his trade when serving in the Royal Navy. He rose through the ranks, serving on some famous ships to become a Sub-Lieutenant before being demobbed. After his time on the Hood and Arc Royal, his friends used to say that ships were sunk every time after he was posted to another ship. Stan also told me that he had served on an American battleship. The Texas in which Robert Mitchum served as an officer, referred to by Stan as a 'true gentleman'. This ship has been restored and is on show in the port of Atlanta, Georgia. Reference is made of this in the History Society's first book, 'Distington the Friendly Parish'. Stan's house was named 'Twin Elms', after the two trees in the garden. It stood overlooking the Loop Road. It was badly damaged by fire on 21st July 2007. Frankie Farr took over to run the bakery after the death of Stan and Madge Grant. The shop was knocked down on Tuesday, 18th March 2003. The ground floor building stones were quarried from the sandstone works of Casson's Quarry.

Tony Graham started up his hairdressing business at no 101 in 1964 before later moving to No 111, into the front room of his house in 1966. He then moved on to Workington. Tony and his son Mark have now gone on to develop the business and own ten shops in West Cumbria and in Lancaster. Bill Foster also started up his TV Business in 101 after Tony, before moving to Lowes shop at the corner of Church St. five years later. He then moved into what was the electrical shop of Myers and Bowman's before moving back to Lowes Corner. Tony Rudd had a bric-a-brac shop here as well. Dr Grant held another surgery at No 105. Numbers 113 and 115 were rebuilt into one shop by Mrs S E (Cissie) Tinnion. She ran a draper's and wool shop. In the

Stan Grant's shop before and after demolition

1940s, Cissie started selling wools and patterns in the kitchenette of her house, number 62 also called Lorne House, before moving into her front room. In a competition for the Festival of Britain celebrations, Cissie's shop was awarded first prize for the best decorated window. In 1953, when the new shop was ready, she moved everything across the road on a Saturday morning and reopened on the Monday morning, expanding the business to include the selling of clothing. She remained in the shop until 1978. Cissie has served on many committees since coming to the village in 1936 after her marriage to Len, including the Parish Council and the Boy's Club for over 50 years.

Mrs Belle Storr was next into the shop. It then became a Delicatessen and was once the Village Chippy, when owned by Frank Farr.

At the rear of No 70, Dryden Hepburn had a boot and shoe repair shop in a small hut. This has also been a chip shop in its time. At the corner of Hinnings Road was Veronica's chip shop. Frank Farr and Christine Atkinson followed. It is now Tony's chip shop. The Central Stores, number 98B, was a greengrocer's shop. A number of owners have run this shop including Gilf Dixon, before he moved over the road adjacent to Ulpha Glebe, at one time a farm. He operated a hardware shop. Mr J Myers was the shop owner in 1951 and was followed by Walter and Julia Bound, Kateels and Colin and Avril Crossfield before it closed in October, 1974. At one time, it was a launderette.

Opposite the store, after Gilf Dixon had left his hardware shop, Mrs Mary Chester ran the Spinning Wheel, selling wools, etc, and then Dorothy Stables used it as a ladies clothing shop. A little further along the road, No 98 D, George Lamby Branthwaite ran a Gent's Hairdressers. He had been there since coming home from the WW I after being seriously wounded. At Prospect Villas, Mrs Roach had a baker's shop.

The Reading Room, number 131 had the village library as well as its other activities and meetings for the benefit of the village. It has now been sold to a private developer for houses. Opposite was Arthur Neen's newsagent's shop, number 106. This was the first joiner's workshop for Myers and Bowman's. Lesley's Hairdresser's salon at the Antelope was once a Public House. Next to Myers and Bowman's car showrooms, at the junction of Prospect View,

stood a house occupied by Jessie Harrison. She collected rosehips for medical requirements.

At Brookside, Common End, opposite Boot public house, there was a builder's yard, run by A Green. Adjacent to No 1 Boot Brow was another fish and chip shop. In the Boot House, an ex pub, Colin McAvoy runs a greengrocer business. At Wellington House was a grocer's shop, run in turn by Isaac Fox and Tom Wilson, followed by Mr Moffatt, Mr Fawcett and Mr Stevenson. The shop closed in 1973. At the top of the hill, opposite Swallow Hill was a shop in the old Albert Hall. Mattie Boyd had a confectionary shop there followed by Arthur Hughes who repaired television sets.

At No 6 Commonside, George Tolson had a dental surgery. Next door at No 5, lived Jim Lowther, who was the village policeman. At No 1 Commonside, Mrs Gunn ran a sweet shop and also sold pies from her front room. All three are now private houses. The Bennett family operated a milk business from their home, Sherwood House, at the southern end of the village. J Weightman now runs the milk business although not in this house. Mrs Jessie McSherry had a shop in the row of terraced houses near the top of Swallow Hill.

Off Main Street, at No 1 Chapel Street, Horace (Cow) Wilson had a greengrocer's shop. A winch could be seen over the upstairs door where stock was lifted up to the storeroom. At 17 Church Road, Billy Bell repaired bicycles from a shed at the back of his house. This house is now a hydrotherapy unit. On Kilnside, at No 12, now No 8, Hetty Patterson sold sweets from her front room. When she closed down, Bertha Birkett, who lived at No 16, now No 12, started up to do the same thing. When Kilnside was built, numbers 1 to 12 were numbered 5 to 16. Numbers 1 to 4 were the two semi-detached houses around the corner on Church Road. Jack Bell lived at 78 Barffs Road, now No 8. He was a market gardener and sold vegetables from his horse and cart. Arthur Dempster of Glebe Road had a vehicle repair workshop beside the Barffs Quarry at the rear of 28 Barffs Road.

There were a number of shops in Pica. In the 1940s and 1950s, at No 20 was Bobby Cass. He had a window display, sold sweets, etc. and made his own ice-cream. Customers could sit down in his front room and he always enjoyed a crack. He also ran a parcels office for Cumberland Motor Services.

Festival of Britain Queen, Ivy Watson 1951. Attendants: Elizabeth Halley, Maud Brough, & Nora Robinson.

The Cleator Moor Co-operative Society store was managed by Steven Whiteside and was at No 28. This was Branch No 20, and sold everything from groceries to footwear. The village Post Office was in different places over the years and was also a general stores shop. At 59, it was run by Mr Blenkinsopp. He had two table tops for his counter and also sold a small amount of tobacco. Ernie Beverley was next at No 87, followed by Albert and Phyllis Jackson at 73. It was also a small general store. After this, Jennifer Metherell had the Post Office at No 65. Etta Penrice sold sweets and confectionary from the front room of her house. At No 52, Elizabeth Bawden did the same thing, selling from the lobby of her house. This closed down in 1940. Pica Miners Welfare sold ice-cream.

Into the 21st century, there are no shops left in Pica and the only shops in Distington are the newsagents, the Co-operative, Foster's Car Radio repairs, Post Office, Delicatessen and Tony's Chippie, plus the Lamb's coal yard, Lynda's hairdressing business and the Antelope hairdressing salon. Only two pubs remain open, The Globe and The Castle.

Distington celebrated the Coronation of Queen Elizabeth II on the 2nd June, 1953. On Sunday 30th March, 1953, the Reverend Charles Warren, Rector of the Church of the Holy Spirit, held a special church service. The following day, a Coronation Ball was held in the Enterprise Ballroom. Margaret Turner, of Main Street, won the title of 'Miss Coronation' and was presented with a signet ring by the chairman of the committee. Attendants were Ann Lennon, Valerie Quayle, Dorothy Anderson and Nora Robinson.

A carnival was held on Coronation Day. A colourful procession formed in the Pond Field, where the Community Centre is now. It toured the streets of the village, going along Barffs Road to the Main Road, past Millyard and through the main street until finishing in Hayescastle Field, Common End, also known in my time as Brayton's field. A programme of sporting events then took place.

MYERS AND BOWMAN'S

The story of Myers and Bowman's years in business was told to me by the late Maurice Boyd.

Myers and Bowman's garage was probably the best known in Cumberland and the North of England for heavy vehicle repairs. Bill Myers and Billy Bowman started repairing and selling cycles and small farm machinery in the Greyhound Pub Pica run by John Myers, Bill's father. The two men were brothers-in-law; Billy Bowman had married Ada Myers. The pub was run as a family business. Billy Myers had served his time as an apprentice electrician. He worked for T S Bells of Tangier Street, Whitehaven. Billy Bowman was an engineer. He was taught his trade at Lowca Foundry, run by Fletcher Jennings. Cameron Boyd, who worked with him at the foundry, joined in the business when work was expanding. Cameron later married Isobel, one of the Myers sisters.

During the First World War, Billy Myers joined the Royal Flying Corps as a pilot. On his return from the Forces, Billy bought his first car from the Argyle Garage in Whitehaven after seeing all the bits lying in a storeroom. He assembled it at his home, the Greyhound pub at Pica. Billy then bought an American Maxwell chassis and engine. He fitted a body of a horse drawn cart to the chassis, complete with seating. He then ran a bus service from Pica to Whitehaven. Billy later bought an aeroplane in kit form and assembled it himself with the Boyd family. When flying around, it was known as the 'Flying Flea'.

By 1921, the business was getting too big for the Greyhound pub. They rented a barn on Main Street Distington, owned by Katie Fleming and tenanted by the Kirkpatrick family, who were farming in the village. The site of this barn is at the present Rathbones Workshop, and was for many years the showrooms for the new cars to be sold. The number of the farmhouse was 114, and is now the home of

Doris Calvin, the daughter of Ada Bowman. Bill and Ada Bowman occupied and ran the Hope and Anchor public house next door to 114. Isobel and Cameron Boyd tenanted the Greyhound public house. Billy and Dora Myers built a house behind the Reading Room and overlooking the Loop Road, now occupied by Stuart Grant.

In 1924, they started to sell Chevrolet and Buick cars. In the early 1930s, the firm took on Jack Casson, a joiner who lived in Distington. As the number of cars increased, so did the workshops. A heavy vehicle workshop was built along with the joiner's shop which had started up in 106 Main St, opposite the Reading Room, electrical workshops and paint shops were also built. They became agents for Chevrolet, Reo, Bedford, Hillman, Humber and Sunbeam Talbot cars. They also became the agents for selling and servicing fuel injector pumps for all diesel engines.

When Billy Myers and Billy Bowman wanted to expand with a joinery workshop, they recruited John (Jack) Casson, who already had his own business as a joiner and undertaker on the main street. Jack became the third director and took responsibility for the coachwork and for the undertaking departments. His grandson, John Lace served his time with him. Ronnie Rogerson ran the undertaking business in the 1960s. Myers and Bowman were skilled at building bodies on to chassis to customer's requirements. The workshops were increased for the Ministry of Defence, referred to as the M O D, and also for a black-smith's workshop and a coach building workshop. The buildings were supplied with electrical power from their own generating room. It was powered by two Blackstone horizontal engines and a Harland and Wolf air blast injection engine driving 110 volt dynamos. These were known as 'Cameron's Motors'. With the start of WW II, contracts were obtained from the M O D for the maintenance of military vehicles. The company

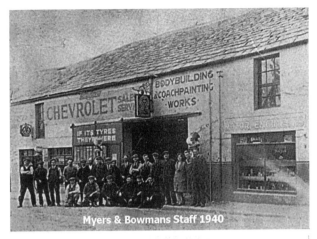

Myers & Bowmans Staff 1940

Billy Myers

was re-organised during the war, working 7 days per week and 12 hours per day. Many of the workers were women. After the war, the premises were extended to build their own vehicles. They bought Commer vehicle chassis. A driver would go down to the Midlands to pick up a chassis. The chassis was completed mechanically and could be driven. The drivers sat on a seat in the open, regardless of the weather and brought it to Distington. Specialised bodies were built, including various commercial vehicles, fire engines, ambulances and buses for Cumberland Motor Services Ltd. These were typical of the vehicles delivered. The vehicle sales included Foden, ERF, Commer and Leyland, including the famous Comet range. Billy Bowman died in 1941. After World War II 80 men were employed in the works. After the war, the telephone numbers were Harrington 247, 248 and 249.

A service workshop operated on Vulcans Lane, Workington, opposite the rear entrance to the bus station and ran from 1962 to 1982. A showroom was used on Finkle Street, Workington. This also closed in 1982. The coach and repair workshops in Distington closed and were knocked down in 1981. The Old Coachworks Depot is now used by Tyson Burridge Transport Company. Myers and Bowman's now operate a car showroom dealership at Lillyhall.

The Enterprise Ballroom was built above the electrical stores and entrance was by a flight of stone steps outside of the ballroom, at the southern end of the building, the only entrance at that time. Ladies and Gents cloakrooms were at each side of the entrance door. The stage was at the works end of the room. The Ballroom was opened by the Doctors, Mr & Mrs Watson of Attorgarth, Common End in 1935. Dancing was very popular. A band played every week, no recorded music then. The band during the war was the Swingstars with regular musicians the Belford brothers of Lowca, Peter and Tommy Coyles and Aaron Coates on the drums. Later Bob Corlett of Kilnside became drummer. On one occasion at Christmas time, the band members walked to Moresby Miners Welfare club to play from midnight to four in the morning, They then walked to the coal mine at Lowca to start work on day shift, allowing only a few hours sleep. There were no dances allowed by law to take place on Sundays or Christmas Day.

The company opened the Enterprise Cinema on Tuesday, 21st November 1944. Ada Bowman,

Billy's widow, and Jack Casson became the directors of the cinema. At the same time, Ada was licensee of the Hope and Anchor pub. The opening film was 'Coney Island', starring Betty Grable. The arcs of the projectors required plenty of electrical power. The 110 Volt DC supply from 'Cameron's Motors' was used and the stage was moved to the Main Street end of the ballroom. A new entrance was built giving access from Main Street. The first projectionist was Norman Palfreyman. Mrs Hilda Corlett and Caddie Ward took turns each week issuing tickets. Maurice Boyd took over the projectionist duties in 1946 after returning from the army at the end of the WW II. George Cheek, ex RAF, also worked with Maurice and became a projectionist. The normal showings were every Tuesday, Thursday and Saturday at 6pm and 8.15pm. Admission was 1/9d, (7½p), 1 shilling (5p), and 10 pence (4p). The 10 pence seats were the first five rows, quite close to the screen but when they were full, children sat on the floor. The popularity of cinema finished with the development of television. The last two films to be shown were, 'I was Monty's Double', staring John Mills and Cecil Parker, a war time story shown on Thursday 30th July and on the final Saturday the film was 'She Didn't Say No', a comedy staring Eileen Herlie and Niall MacGinnis. The Enterprise Cinema closed down on 1st August 1959.

Cameron Boyd's two sons Maurice, born April, 1915 at Foundry Road Parton, and his brother John, went to school at Pica. They then became apprentices with Myer's & Bowman Company and later salesmen. Both were called up for War Service. John joined the RAF, Maurice joined the RAC (Royal Armoured Corp) as a mechanic.

Maurice was in the British Expeditionary Force, sent to France, landed at Marseilles and rode around on a motorcycle with his Regiment, until Germany invaded and he then made his way to Dunkirk. Maurice had the worst experience of his life when on the beaches of Dunkirk in May 1940, standing up to his neck in the sea, loaded with full kit and rifle and he could not swim. In the queue to get on a rescue ship, he was stopped just six feet short of getting on board. As he watched the boat leaving, it was attacked and sunk. He was able to get on the next boat, a Royal Navy destroyer, and returned to England. His family had not heard from him for months until he got to Dover and was able to phone home. He was then transferred to the REME and

Officers Training School in Dunbar, East Lothian Scotland in charge of transport. The family lived near the harbour. The Army asked him to go to Germany after the war as part of the Army of Occupation but he declined. Both brothers were demobbed in 1945 and returned to the company.

After the war, the business continued to be a family concern. Bill Myer's two sons, John and Kit, daughter Sylvia and Cameron Boyd's sons, Maurice and John, ran the company. Maurice took control of the engine house and looked after Cameron's Motors. They generated their own electricity for all of the works. As well as working as the cinema projectionist in the evenings, Maurice worked on the building of Calder Hall, installing and maintaining generators. At Whitehaven Harbour, he maintained the pilot boat and coasters (small ships), and he installed mechanical engine-driven pumps at Workington docks. He enjoyed working on anything mechanical all his life.

While continuing to work at Myers & Bowman's, he moved to take over the Wheatsheaf Pub in Flimby in 1962. On his retirement, Maurice and his wife bought Ivy Cottage, Flimby, in 1967 and later moved back to Distington. Maurice remained active. He was a lifetime member of the Melbreak Foxhounds, a member of the Harrington Sailing Club, and a member of the Vintage Rally Club for 23 years. 2004 was the first year he missed. At the age of 84, he fell off a tandem with his son Michael in Singapore. He was still driving his car until he had a stroke in Feb 2004 and died in July, 2004, aged 89.

John Boyd joined Myers and Bowman's in 1932. He served with the RAF from 1939 to 1946, rising to the rank of Squadron-Leader, (Engineering Officer). When he retired, he was President of the British Legion and President of the Boy's Club.

Maurice's son Michael became an apprentice into the company in 1955. After completing his apprenticeship in 1960, he joined the Merchant Navy as an engineer on a cargo ship. He left the Merchant Navy to become underground engineer at Risehow Colliery, Flimby. When this pit closed, he then worked in the gold mines of South Africa. He now lives in Kent.

John Myers and Ada Bowman were joint managing directors until Ada's death in 1973. With the retirement of Maurice and John Boyd by 1982, the business was run by Raymond and Doris Calvin, Ada Bowman's daughter. After Raymond's death, it is now run by their sons, Graham and Steven Calvin,

The sales of the Roote's Group cars, Hillman, Humber, Sunbeam Talbot, Singer and Chrysler have ended. Today the sales are of Peugeot and Toyota. The Myers and Bowman's name was advertised on the 'Dragonfly' railway bridge. The advert was for Dragonfly engine oils.

The workshops of the Old Coach Works, Main Street were knocked down in 1981 and now many different firms use the yard. The showrooms were kept and the company continued to sell cars. A new showroom was built at Toll Bar at the junction of the road to High Harrington. This was opened in 1992.

J S CROOKDAKE & SONS

John Salkeld Crookdake opened a blacksmith's forge in the early 1800s. The forge and workshop was on Pandora Terrace, Main Street, opposite what is now the paper shop. Its main work at the turn of the century was to make new iron shoes for heavy shire carthorses working on the local farms. They also repaired equipment belonging to the many farms in the district. The forge continued in use until after WW II. I can still remember it working when I was a school boy. The heat of the forge fire kept an iron shelf beside an open window hot enough to be handy for local people to use when baking bread. The forge closed down in the late 1940s.

In the 1920s, the firm moved across the road and became motor engineers. A workshop was opened to repair cycles and motor-cycles. In 1928, the company was advertised as John S Crookdake. Blacksmith and Motor cycle dealer. The telephone number was given as Harrington 6. They were the sole agents for B S A, New Hudson and Raleigh motor cycles. In later years, they continued repairing any vehicle as required. When his two sons, Stan and John joined him, they traded as J S Crookdake and Sons. Stan Crookdake was a mechanic and his brother John was an electrician. They ran the garage for many years maintaining vehicles from the village. They sold petrol, oils and paraffin. They had a franchise to sell Austin, Morris, Riley and MG cars, all part of the British Motor Company (BMC) Group. They still sold the occasional motor cycle. I bought my first new motorbike from them, a 1954 BSA with a 249 cc side valve engine, number NRM 858. It was brand new and cost £114.

In wartime when electricity was unreliable, many people had a 'wireless' set, powered by a 6 volt battery. These batteries were taken to the garage to be re-charged. The garage was extended in 1953, when the rear half was built on where the hoist is now. Timber and roof slates were bought when the Poor House was knocked down at Brewery Brow, Parton. Stan died on the 27th Jan 1969 aged 59. John sold the business in 1971 to two mechanics working there, Russell Grant and John Briggs, who had both served their time working in the garage. In 1991, the three petrol pumps, which were used to sell two star, three star and four star grades of petrol, had to be removed when EEC regulations prevented garages from selling petrol to vehicles standing on the road. A forecourt was required with pumps set back then became the law. At the turn of the new century, this was the only garage still trading in the village for mechanical repairs. Stan's wife, Marjorie owned a shop on Pow St, Workington known as Workington Weatherware.

National Benzole pump

Another member of the Crookdake family was Tom Crookdake. He became a police inspector in Shanghai. On his retirement, he returned to Distington and built a house on the road to Gilgarran, just below the present Crematorium and named it 'Mo in Shan', a Chinese name. It is now named 'Birkwood', probably changed by Dr Calder, when he lived there. After the death of Tom, his widow lived in Church Road.

John Crookdake Senior, John Crookdake Junior and a customer

Jack Mitchell, Stan Crookdake and Leonard Tinnion

Stan (left) and his dad John Crookdake

HIGH DUTY ALLOYS

Information regarding the history of the High Duty Alloys Limited came from the late Gilbert Rothery, a good friend of my dad when they worked together for many years.

In the mid 1920s in Slough, Bucks, Colonel Wallace Charles Devereux decided to build the High Duty Alloys, known throughout the country as the HDA. Col Devereux, or 'Dev' as most of his colleagues knew him, was born in 1893. He had studied metallurgy and engineering. After this came a short term in the army before he moved on to be a superintendent in an aircraft factory during World War I.

The factory that Dev worked for closed down on 5th January 1927. The newly Registered Company of High Duty Alloys came into operation on 5th January 1928. Mr H G Herrington joined the company in 1930 and became General Manager in 1937. He was appointed Managing Director after the war. An agreement with John Siddeley, later the 1st Lord Kenilworth, gave Dev the money to start up. A Rolls Royce order in 1929 allowed the HDA to spread worldwide. The Company got a world licence for manufacturing Rolls Royce aluminium. RR 77 was developed which was three times harder than carbon steel. It was registered in its trade name of Hiduminium RR 77. Then the HDA started to develop lightweight metals such as magnesium.

The first factory was built on the Trading Estate on Farnham Road, Slough. A second factory was built in Redditch, Worcester when Slough was unable to expand any further and it was opened by Sir Kingsley Wood who was Secretary of State for Air on Wed 16th August 1939. At the beginning of World War II, a shadow factory was planned for the north.

The chairman of the West Cumberland Development Company, Jack Adams, persuaded them to use the site of Lillyhall Farm, covering an area of 50 acres. The remains of the former Distington Iron Works, with its railway line were an added attraction. John Laing and Son Ltd. of Carlisle began to build the new factory in mid February 1940 in the middle of the worst winter since 1895.

The Redditch factory had a heavy hammer called an Erie hammer and the vibrations were shaking the foundations very badly. It could have destroyed the building. The Distington factory had a smaller hammer called a Massey hammer. The solid clay base of Lillyhall Farm was much more suited to the hammering so the Air Ministry in a meeting on 7th October 1941, decided to swap these hammers. The Erie hammer remained the property of the crown for the duration of the war but the Ministry agreed the following expenditure:-

1	New anvil block for Erie hammer	£6,400
2	Foundation for Erie hammers at Distington	£5,000
3	Erection of compressor building at Distington	£2,600
4	Erection of Erie hammer at Distington	£2,500
5	Transportation of Erie hammer to Distington	£5,000
6	Electric cable and equipment at Distington	£5,000
	Sundry items	£500
	Total	**£27,000**

The Air Ministry paid HDA £6,000 for the consideration of exchanging hammers. It was also agreed that HDA would pay for the installation of the new block for the Erie hammer.

The hammer weighed 45 tons and was brought up to Distington on a trailer hauled by three steamrollers, travelling at five miles per hour and pushed by another. The route diverted the load to avoid the bombed areas of Lancashire and used the A6 road over Shap. An accident happened when the load of the steamrollers and trailer became too much for a railway bridge, which collapsed and blocked the line for four days. The hammer, when installed in 1942 was operated by waterpower with 2,000 tons of pressure. The noise of the hammer working could be heard all over the village on a summer's night.

The factory had its own 10,000 KVA substation, gas purifying plant, their own gasholder holding one third of a million cubic feet and its own reservoir pumping station. A large water tank on a tower at roof top height, holding 40,000 gallons was built among the trees to the north of the factory.

The first engineers, operators and apprentices were trained up at Moss Bay Steel works, with assistance from the Technical College Workington, to be ready for when the factory came into production. HDA hired workshops for a temporary tool room from Myers and Bowman's at their Prospect garage. The first extruded bar, two inches in diameter, of Hiduminium RR56, was produced on 16th January 1941, using the 2,000 ton 'Hamilton' extrusion press, one of three set up for the workload. At its peak in 1943, over 3,500 people worked there during the war. Many of these were women recruited when men were called up to the military services. By 1943, over two million tons of aluminium had been made which was more than the total for the rest of the world.

Various parts of aircraft engines were made for Rolls Royce and for Hadley Page Ltd for the Halifax Bomber. Foundry output was 3,000 tons of cast metal. Forged were 2,000 propeller blades, 6,000 crankcases, 40,000 cylinder barrels and 1,000,000 general components. Extrusion produced 1,600 tons of forged bar and sections. At the end of the war, Dev resigned and Hugh G. Herrington took over control of the HDA. Ironically, a second Erie hammer had been made and was in Eastern Europe. When the Germans took control of it, they made the same parts for their aircraft.

After the war, the market requirements changed. The work-force was reduced to 1,000. Aluminium was supplied for prefabs, which were expected to

last until 1980. Many lasted much longer than this. Milk churns were popular, as were parts for car radiators. The HDA was re-organised, Distington becoming the Extrusion Division, Slough becoming the Castings Division and Redditch the Forging Division. Two more water presses were added, a 2,000 ton and a 3,000 ton water press. The Korean War also brought new orders when propeller driven aircraft engines were replaced by jet-engines. Much harder metals were then required.

In the 1960s, plans were announced for a new aeroplane, the Concorde passenger aeroplane. Aluminium was needed to be made of much higher standard than before. New presses of 1,250 tons and 2,750 tons were bought, followed by a press of 1,600 tons to obtain the satisfactory levels. The new alloy for the wings of the Concorde was Hiduminium RR58.

In 1975, Hawker Siddeley Group split up the different factories into individual groups. The Lillyhall factory became High Duty Alloys Extrusions Ltd from 1 January 1976. In March 1979, the company was taken over by British Aluminium Company Ltd. This Company then merged with Alcan Aluminium (UK) Ltd and changed its name to Alcan High Duty Extrusions Ltd. The HDA was modernised and a new 'Orion' press was bought, a greatly improved quality machine. During this year the 'Queen's Award to Technical Industry' was awarded to HDA.

The Foundry was at the rear of the works. Aluminium was made and heated in furnaces before being poured into mould to create ingots. A large chimney stood outside the northern end of the foundry. It stood 256 feet high and was called a Jacobite chimney because of the rotary furnace, used to melt scrap metal, at its base. Fumes were channelled up the chimney. It was demolished circa 1979. A specialist crew erected wooden ladders up the side of the chimney, hammering iron supports into the brickwork. The ladders were hung on these supports. They then started to dismantle the chimney brick by brick, dropping them down the centre of the chimney. A hole was opened up in the side of the chimney at ground level to clear out these bricks.

The HDA has done its part in looking after the children of its workers. A large Christmas party regularly took place over many years in the staff canteen. The works staff put on a pantomime every year. The canteen was also used to entertain the Reunion Club old-age pensioners in the village. HDA bought Moresby Hall to look after visitors to the factory.

A story handed down from the war years tell of a French Canadian, when working in the foundry, needed somewhere to live after being turned out of his lodgings. He set up a pile of boxes in a corner of the foundry and brought in a bed. He had access to washing places and the canteen. He was well known by the police on the gate so he could come and go as he wanted. He lived like this for many months.

A new sports club and playing field was set up and opened in 1969. This was funded by workers and supported by HDA. Goal posts and rugby posts were donated by HDA.

In 1971, the '30 Years Club' was set up. It was open to every member of HDA staff who had completed 30 years employment with the company. This club is still active, even though HDA is no longer there.

About 1995, the Luxor Group bought the works, then British Alcan, and in April 2001, the French company, Pechenay became the next owners. In January, 2002, 70 men at the works took early retirement or redundancy to leave less than 200 still working at the plant. The works were again owned by Alcan when they bought out Pechenay. The production workers were finally paid off on 27th April 2007 leaving only enough staff left to dismantle the machinery.

Small businesses moved into some of the vacant sheds at the northern end of the factory buildings when the factory closed down.

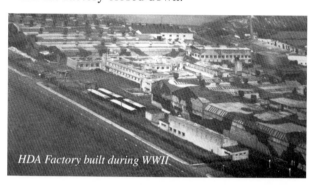

HDA Factory built during WWII

SCOUTS

The Boys Scout Brigade was first set up in 1907 by Lord Baden-Powell, a retired Army Officer, who had made his name in South Africa during the Boer War. Commissioners for the scouts were appointed for areas throughout the country. Scouts were known to be active in Distington in 1928.

In 1961, the 1st troop of Distington was formed. Don Scarrott of Commonside became the scout leader, followed by Jack Murray and Norman Jeffries of Hayescastle Road. Ray Daniels was the leader of the Cubs. During Don's time as leader, Bill Richardson of Church Road rose to become a Queen's Scout.

Here are Don Scarrott's memories of those days.

Beginnings

1961 saw the start of the 1st Distington Scout Group. Meetings were held in the church hall, and during the winter Saturday afternoons, we would go for a short hike and cook some food on a wood fire. We visited Prospect, Hinnings and Gooseberry Hill woods and also went to the Harrington and Micklam shores. I don't know how much the boys learned, but I had to light fires under all sorts of conditions.

My old scout troop used to have a proper 'Trek-Cart'. This was a light wooden platform on two light wooden wheels, with a pole at the front. This made it easy to carry the heavy camp gear. A local garage offered to make us one but only had a couple of motorbike wheels. These were not too bad, and we did have the advantage of pneumatic tyres, but instead of a high platform, we ended up with something more like a large box. The result was it was rather heavy and unwieldy, but we loaded it up and set off for our first camp. It was quite a slog up the hills to Tuthill, but we all pulled together and the effort of getting there made us feel as though

we had achieved something. Nowadays, we use motorised transport without thinking about it, and travel further.

Quite soon we acquired a second hand hut from Sellafield construction site, and erected it in Maddock's field beside the houses on Chapel Street. Meetings were held there for many years, but eventually it burnt down.

Canoeing

We built ourselves a sturdy two man canvas canoe and took it to several camps. This was a 'touring' type with a keel, which keeps it going straight. However, we also used the canoe facilities at Hawes End on Derwentwater Lake. This allowed all the boys to paddle their own 'slalom' canoe. These are made without a keel for manoeuvrability, but this makes it difficult to keep them going a straight line, so beginners spent much time keeping together.

We had one memorable exercise to find some buried treasure on one of the islands. The boys of course, operated as two patrols and there was a competition between them to see who could win the most points. The 'Treasure' was a tin containing boiled sweets. As I did not want the papers left around, there was a point to be gained for each paper returned. Inevitably, some boys did not pay attention, but I was agreeably surprised to hear one patrol leader telling off and sending them back to recover the sweet papers before the other patrol found them.

Ashness Bridge

The Keswick group have a camp site at Ashness Bridge and one year, we went to camp there. The site is about 100 yards above the road, on a patch of ground not quite as steep as the rest of the hill. There is a nice stream on one side and a green hut on the other. The door faces the stream and while one end rests on the rocky ground, the other is raised a few feet to keep it level. My wife had come along to lend a hand and she was to sleep in the hut. I believed that the scoutmaster should share the same conditions as the boys, so I was to sleep in my own little tent. The effort of carrying all the kit up from the road and setting up camp tired everybody out, so the boys went to sleep quite quickly for once. I woke at one o'clock to find it had started to drizzle. I got up to check that everything was under cover and popped my head into the hut door to see if everything was all right. Eva had her head under the bedclothes and was shivering with fear. The floor moved she said. I moved in beside her to keep her company and just as I was drifting off, the floor DID move and there was a clanking from below. I shot down to the end of the hut and shone my torch under the hut to see a pair of green eyes glaring at me. It was one of the local sheep taking shelter from the rain.

The next day we were preparing dinner, and one of the boys told to peel the potatoes complained bitterly. He was an only child and somewhat spoilt, but in camp he was not going to get away with it and was forced to do his duty and help with the cooking. Later that day, his parents came to visit and he went down to see them. I happened to hear his mother ask solicitously if he wanted to come back home and was much surprised to hear him say NO very firmly. He was apparently enjoying it after all.

Backwoodsman Badge

Joe decided that he wanted to take the Backwoodsman Badge. This required building a shelter and cooking a bird in clay. We managed to get a chicken complete with feathers and all, and set off for a weekend camp at Ennerdale.

The Ennerdale campsite is well provided with reeds and these can be tied to a pole framework to make a very serviceable shelter, but it needs many helpers to collect the reeds, so we all helped to collect the materials and Joe did eventually produce a shelter. It can shed the water quite well, and is very cosy inside.

Each kitchen area needs a wet pit to dispose of the dirty water and we found that as we went deeper, we got into a band of clay. Though not very good for a wet pit, it was just what we needed for cooking the bird, so we used a tin to scrape the clay out down as far as an arm would reach and stored it until the Sunday morning. Then we lit a fire. You need a lot of embers for his purpose and Joe duly cleaned out the bird, and thereafter was always known as 'Giblets'. Anyway, the wind was getting up. It was blowing straight down the lake and the tents were in danger off taking off, so we hurriedly covered the bird in a good layer if clay, and dumped it in the fire while we struck camp. The wind fanned the flames and it blazed away like a furnace.

The camp warden turned up just as we had finished packing, and we were able to offer him a nicely cooked chicken leg. The other one had burnt off through a crack in the clay due to the unceremonious dumping. Now, he went to check if the wet pits were wet enough by poking a stick into them, and took me to one side and said 'How did you get the pit so deep?'

After Don retired from the scouts, Jim Murray of Distington Park took over, followed in turn by Norman Jeffries of Common End. In 1972. Norman took the troop to a Jamboree at Southend. The troop won all eight of the competitions during this event, winning £250, much to the disgust of the German scouts who had been confident of winning everything. The scouts made use of Cumbrian dialect words to confuse anyone who cared to listen.

Unfortunately, this was also the last of the Boy Scout Movement in Distington as Norman resigned to give more time to his work and nobody took over in his place.

Cub Scouts in the village were run for 30 years by Ray Daniels of Hayescastle Road. He took boys aged up to 11 years and held meetings in the Church Rooms, Boy's Club rooms and the Coronation Hall. They finished when Ray had to retire at the age of 65 in 1995 and there was nobody else to take over from him.

GUIDES

Girl Guides have been very active in the parish. The Guides were formed by Lady Baden-Powell in 1910; three years after Lord Baden-Powell had formed the scout movement. The organisation was on similar lines. Like the scouts, the guides were very active in the 1920s.

Mrs Mary Canfield wrote this account of her memories of her years in the Guides.

The Guides were revived in 1956 by Mrs Sowden, the wife of the rector. There had been Guides as early as the 1920s when the Guider (Captain) walked to Distington from Gilgarran. I was a Guide from 1947 to 1949 when our Captain was Miss Daisy Hodgson and Miss May Patterson was a Lieutenant. We never went camping, but we used to go onto the old line and cook. We sang a lot, learned Morse code and played things like 'Kim's Game'. When May got married, the Guides formed a Guard of Honour at the church.

In 1949, we went to a rally at Carlisle to see Lady Baden-Powell. She certainly had charisma and I will never forget how impressed I was. I took over from Mrs Elsie Coady in 1970. I had just gone to help out with a few crafts, but Elsie took ill and I inherited them. I had to take tests before I got a warrant and I had to go for training to get a Camper's licence. We used to camp at various places in the Lake District, but we used the scout's campsite at Branthwaite a lot. One of our Guides, Barbara Allan, became a Queen's Guide, which was very difficult and entailed a lot of work. Mrs Margaret Thorpe, the wife of the village policeman, was assistant Guider until they moved, and she took over a Whitehaven company. I gave up the Guide Company about 1998, but continued with the Rainbows until 2001, when I retired after 30 years.

Mrs Sowden also started the Brownies with Pat Barwise as 'Brown Owl'. She was followed by Jean

Halley, Eileen Gregson and then in about 1970 by Mrs Eileen Porter. Mrs Janet Hall is the Brownie Guider now.

In 1988, I started up the Rainbow Guides (aged 5-7) with Mrs Rose Franklin, the wife of the village policeman at that time. Janet Hall followed and then Lynda Elliot. Rainbows and Brownies are still flourishing but there are no Guides at the moment.

Barbara Allen, then aged 15, was awarded the Queen's Guide Badge on 14 June 1972, in the Church Hall on Church Road. She was presented with the badge by Miss M Rattrie, the Divisional Commissioner. Barbara was the first Girl Guide to be given this award in the South Workington District.

Barbara Allan pictured receiving her Queen's Guide Award. Courtesy of Workington News & Star

South Workington District's first Queen's Guide, Barbara Allen, of Distington, shows her badge display to the Divisional Commissioner, Miss M. Rattrie (left) and the Distington Guider, Mrs E. M. Canfield, after she had received her award last week. Barbara, aged 15, is a pupil at Whitehaven Grammar School.

BROWNIES

This is an account of the Brownies by Jean Nicholson, nee Halley.

Pat Barwise started the Brownies in Distington in February 1959. Mrs Sowden, the wife of the vicar at the time, was the District Commissioner for Whitehaven and she was also the leader of the village Guides. I do not think there had been a Brownie group in the village before. Christine Collins was one of Pat's first helpers. She was a Guide and you had to be enrolled as a Guide before you could be a leader. Joan Quayle and I were asked to help Pat. I was enrolled as a Guide and then took my warrant to be Tawny Owl.

Pat left to go to teacher's training college in 1961. I took over as Brown Owl and ran the pack with the help of Eileen Gregson who was Tawny Owl until 1967, when I got married and went to live in Canada.

In the beginning the pack met every Tuesday evening in the old Church Hall. When Pat left, the evening was changed to Fridays and by then we were in the new spacious Church Hall, which had a lot more facilities. We were now under the Workington District Guides and all the Guiders from surrounding groups met once a month to discuss District business and group news. During my time as Brown Owl, our District Commissioner was Mrs Sanderson, the wife of Mr T Sanderson, the Managing Director of the Steel Works. We met at her house in High Harrington. We then had a County Commissioner over the Districts and they reported to headquarters in London.

The Brownies joined when they were seven and left to join the Guides if they wanted to at the age of eleven. The maximum number of girls you could have in a pack was twenty-four.

Each evening we met, we played games, worked toward challenge badges and did craft work. We had to have outside assessors to test and award the Brownies their challenge badges. These would be people in the village who had a particular skill or interest, for instance cooking, sewing or basic first aid.

We had Brownie Revels. On one Saturday every year, Brownies from the District would get together for fun, games and competitions. One year it was in Curwen Park Workington. We also had parents evenings once a year when we invited the Mums and Dads to come along and see what we did and entertain them. Once we had a Maypole dance and Margaret Steele spent weeks training the Brownies to do it without getting all tangled up. Not an easy task but thanks to Margaret's good teaching and patience we had a successful evening. If I remember correctly we even performed a play that night. We had Church Parade once a month, when the Cubs, Guides and Scouts also attended. Each group carried their flags and pennants up to the altar at the beginning of the service and then collected them at the end. It was quite an honour to be chosen to carry the Brownie pennant

When Pat was Brown Owl she took tests to gain her campers licence and was then able to take the

Brownies on holiday. Brownies were not allowed to camp in tents so when they went away they hired Church Halls or School Halls. I only went with them once to Haverigg. Windermere was another place they had a pack holiday. When we went to Haverigg all the camp beds and equipment was transported in Mr Ernie Lamb's furniture van. Eileen Gregson and I and some other girls, who went to help, travelled in the back of the van, it was very dark. The Brownies went on the train with Pat and Mrs Sowden. It was a good week and something I will always remember. We took 17 and it was quite a responsibility. We never lost any.

When I got married at Distington Church, we had a Brownie guard of honour. We still have the photograph where all the Brownies surround us on the steps of the church. One holding the pendant with 'Lend a hand' printed on it, which of course was the Brownie motto. I kept my interest in Brownies and finished my guiding career after 10 years with a Brownie pack in Little Aston in the Midlands.

Brownie Heather Graves (age 8)
Courtesy of Workington News & Star

WOMEN'S INSTITUTE

The Women's Institute was first set up in Canada in 1897 and arrived in West Cumberland about 1915.

A Women's Institute evolved in Distington about this time but activity was shut down during WW II.

The Institute, (WI), re-opened in the village and the first meeting was held in the Reading Room on 14th June 1948. Later meetings were held in the Enterprise Ballroom. Mrs Singleton became President.

In 1959/1960, the President was Mrs S E Tinnion and the Vice Presidents were Miss C Ward and Mrs B Storr. The Secretary was Mrs E Bruce with Mrs Watson as Assistant Secretary. Mrs King was Treasurer. Others on the committee were Mrs H Corlett, Mrs Elliot, Mrs Gillam, Mrs A Bowman, Miss M Holiday, Mrs A Boyd, Mrs C Boyd, Mrs M Grant and Mrs Singleton. It was normal to refer to each other by Mrs or Miss and not by their Christian names. Meetings were held on a monthly basis, the 4th Monday of each month. The membership fee was three shillings and six pence (seventeen and a half pence) per year. The meetings always start with the singing of the hymn, 'Jerusalem', by Robert Blake. This is done nationally throughout the country.

In 1981/82, the President was Mrs Elliot and Mrs Brown was the Vice President. The Secretary was Mrs Marland, the Treasurer was Mrs Izatt and others on the committee were Mrs B Storr, Mrs Casson, Miss C Ward, Mrs M Canfield and Mrs Oldman.

Today the meetings are held in the Community Centre. The President is Mrs A. O'Mahoney. The Secretary is still Mrs Storr and the Treasurer is still Mrs Izatt. At each meeting, there is always a competition and a social half hour. Miss M Steel is the competitions organiser.

MOTHERS' UNION

The Mothers' Union was operating in the 1920s. It was run from the church with many members being in this group as well is the W.I. It is usual for the rector's wife to take a leading role.

At a meeting in November 1928, 52 members enjoyed an afternoon watching a film of the 'Great Societies' work throughout the world. Over 600 members from all over Cumberland came to see the show in Workington. In 1951, 60 members attended another outing.

The present committee has Marlene Pettit as Secretary. It was originally set up for members of the Church of England but other religions have now joined in.

ADULT LEARNING CENTRE

In September 1997, the Adult Learning Centre organised local history sessions in the Community Centre which were led by Maureen Fisher from the Workers' Educational Association. From this, the Distington Local History Society was formed. In the Chair was Nora Lace, the Secretary was Jeff Wilson and then I became Treasurer. Both Marlene Pettit and Anne Shepherd became deputy chairman in their turn. This Society lasted for three years before closing down. There were eighteen members but only six or eight regular members at the end. The list of members during the final year was:–

Nora Lace, the late John Lace, the late Maisie Crossfield, Kath Sharpe, Rose Murray, Blanche Lamb, Caddie Ward, Mervyn Dodd, Jeff Wilson, Ray Daniels and me, Les Nicholson.

The final pay- out of funds went to the Church of the Holy Spirit, the Methodist Chapel, Main St, and the Community Centre. The bank account closed on 6th June 2001. The last AGM was on Monday, 14th May 2001.

The Distington Family History Group was set up and opened after the close down by another group at a meeting organised by the Distington Community Centre leader, Brian Swan on the same day, 14th May 2001. In the chair was Mrs Mary Canfield, the secretary was Gill Foster and the treasurer was Marlene Pettit. After this meeting, two others, Betty Walker and David Foster were co-opted. In 2002, Gill and David Foster left. Mary Canfield became Secretary and I became Chairman.

The society still continues today and in 2006, there were 31 members. The members are Daisy Agnew, Joan Blacklock, May Bone, Mary Canfield, Avril Crossfield, Marjorie and Ray Daniels, Renee Dixon, Shanette and Colin Harding, Margaret Hildrop, June and Norman Jeffries, Nora Lace, Rose Murray, Marlene Pettit, Dora Postletwaite, Reverend Kath Richardson and Malcolm Richardson, Jean Scott, Edith Skillen, Kath Sharpe, Margaret Steele, Caddie Ward, Mary Wilkinson and myself.

I am chairman, Shannette Harding is secretary and Ray Daniels is treasurer.

BOY'S CLUB

The idea of a boy's club came from a group of prisoners of war during World War II. A National Association of Boy's Clubs was set up in 1945. From this, The Cumberland and Westmorland Association of Boy's Clubs was formed. The Whitehaven area was split into 14 sections, from Distington to Gosforth. Mr Arthur Dodd of Distington became the first Chairman. Along with Arthur, Stan Jacks and Austin Robertson-Walker became the main organisers of the Distington Branch.

In 1947, the whole village was invited to a meeting to discus the formation of a new Boy's Club but only five people turned up. The Club was opened in 1948 with Arthur Dodd as Chairman, Stan Jacks as Hon. Sec. and Chris Dixon the school-teacher as Hon. Treasurer. Mrs Cissie Tinnion joined the committee and was still a member in 2005. The Club was to be for boys from 14 to 18 years old, with a limit of 25 members. The Victoria Hall became the club's headquarters and Mr A Tabraham accepted the position of voluntary leader. Grants were given in the first years and membership was increased. The age limit was reduced to 12 for new members. Mr Tabraham resigned at the end of the year.

Sammy Glassford became the next leader. Many events such as dances and fetes were organised to raise money. Weekend courses were held at Irton Hall and Dalston Hall. Mr William Porter of Pica, although handicapped, arranged an appeal and Pica had the honour of being the first village to reach its target. Eventually, enough money was raised to buy its own field, adjacent to the Main St. School. In the mid 1950s, two boys were selected to represent west Cumberland. One came from Maryport and the other was Tony Graham of Distington. Both boys were presented with certificates by Frankie Vaughan, the well known popular singer. This gave Sammy Glassford the chance to invite Frankie Vaughan to open the new club rooms. He accepted. The new clubroom was built in 1956 and officially opened by Frankie Vaughan 22nd October 1958. His popular song at the time, 'Green Door', came from the fact that the doors of all Boy's Clubs at that time were painted green.

On 17th December 1947, Chairman George Tolson of Common End wrote a letter to the people of Distington after he had recently been appointed chairman.

Ladies and Gentlemen,

Although I have only just been appointed chairman of Distington Boy's Club, I have for many years been interested in the boy's club movement and from my experience of the organisation, it is well worthy of public support.

In so much as our club is concerned, I am astonished at the hard work that is being done by the officials, committee and boys alike. Take one activity alone, boxing. The club has produced a champion in John Sisson – a good lad and a credit not only to the club and to his village but to the county. Other good lads have also made their mark. What a grand turn out when Leader Glassford stages a show but what is wanted is more public support.

Help us to erect our own hut, which we so badly need. We are struggling. Once this is accomplished, we shall be on our feet and able to hold our own and provide good entertainment, not only for the boys but for you – the public. I appeal for you all to give generously.

George R Tolson
Chairman

Opening of new Boy's Club by Frankie Vaughan

The club developed promoting many sports. A well-known boxing team in 1952 provided a national champion. Johnny Sisson won his title in London. George Messenger won his local bouts but lost in the Northern Championships in Newcastle. He told me that he got the biggest hiding of his life. Other members of the boxing team included Peter Branthwaite, the Hodgson twins, Dennis and Derek, Colin Crosthwaite and Reg Harrison.

The Boy's Club members were invited to put their thoughts into a booklet produced by the club. Here is one letter.

The Boy's Club as I know it, by Henry Barton

The reason I joined the club was, firstly, because it keeps you out of trouble at night time, secondly, because there are all sorts of games and fun, such as physical training, boxing, table tennis and thirdly, because you meet all your friends and companions there.

I also think that five shillings (25 pence) is a very

reasonable price for a whole year and that half past seven is a good time for the opening of the Boy's Club because it enables any boy at Grammar or the Technical Schools to do their homework in time.

Having football and boxing tournaments, I think it is a very good idea and especially the boxing tournaments have given the club a very good name. I am sure that any boy who attends a boy's club will agree with me that he has spent some very happy evenings in the club.

Distington Boy's Club, of which I am a member, has a fine set of boxers and last year one of them became an English champion. The Boy's Club has its own P T Instructor. On Thursday nights there is a woodwork class for any boy who is keen. Sometimes there are film shows held in the Boy's Club which are very enjoyable. Any boy over the age of twelve may join the club. On Wednesday, there is a Boy's Club night for senior members only. In summer, they make trips to a little cottage in Keswick where they camp for the weekend.

Henry Barton, aged 13 years

The Boy's Club almost closed down in 1983 when the club hut became run down and derelict. A number of people in the village got together and raised £9,000 for the funds, to re-furbish the building. It was re-opened on Tuesday 25th June 1985 by the Lord Lt of Cumbria, Sir Charles Graham. He was the President of the Cumbria Association of Boy's Clubs. The President of the club was John Boyd and the leader was Eddie Neen at this time.

In 1984, the wooden hut was becoming worse for wear. Part of the building had to be taken down for safety reasons. Club Chairman, Stan Jacks made an appeal for £3,000 towards a cost of £20,000 for building a new and better building. Grants and volunteer workers made up the rest. In May 1984, Club leader Eddie Neen, worked with Mike Burns and Ron Wilson, to do the labouring work and with Joe Bennett as site manager, they enlisted the help of several skilled workers to rebuild a more substantial building. It reopened three months later in July 1984. It was also decided to allow girls to join, so the name Boy's Club was changed to the Distington Club for Young People and became a registered charity. The membership of 40 boys and girls now had a new meeting place. The Duke of Gloucester paid a visit to the Boy's Club on 1st May, 1986. There are 90 members today, spread over different ages.

SPORTS

Distington has had a wide variation of sporting activities over many years, going back over many centuries. Men and women have taken part in many sporting events in the village. Pica also contributed to these occasions. Football, cricket, rugby league, hockey and athletics were among the more popular. In 1912, there was also a well attended cycling club.

Grasmere Sports, started in 1865, was and still is a well known event in the north of England. William (Bulger) Branthwaite, of Pica, won the Cumberland and Westmorland Wrestling Championship, wrestling in the 11 stone classes. J McCabe of Distington took part in the Senior Guides race from 1928 to 1933. He finished in second, third and third place again, won in 1931 and then finished in forth place in each of the next two years. He received £1 and a silver cup for winning. Henry Ward took part in the 1965 race.

FOOTBALL

Distington was always known for taking part in sport in the village. The workers of the Distington Iron Works started up the earliest football team, circa 1885. The team was the Lillyhall Wanderers, later to become Distington Football Club. Harry Landells, a man from Kilmarnock, brought his son with him who was able to teach and train the men playing in the team. The first team players were: - Ernest Wilson, Jack McNichol, Bob Withers, Richard Leathers, William Howie, Thomas Hodgson, Harry Landells, Tommy Moore, Joseph Hodgson, Alex Barwick and Charles Wilkinson. Thomas Hodgson was picked to play in the first representative game for Cumberland in 1886. Plains of Airdrie were the visitors who won 5-1. This team played in a small league with Carlisle, Barrow and Workington. A few years later, Arlecdon, Frizington and Millom also joined in the league. Lillyhall then became Distington AFC. At a meeting in the

Commercial Hotel, Workington, on 9th September 1909, the future of Distington football club was discussed by the Cumberland Football Association. There was opposition to Distington remaining in the league because of an old debt to Keswick football club. Distington had been taken over by a new committee and the meeting allowed Distington to remain in the league.

Pica formed a team and played in a field near the Greyhound pub. It was said that many teams and referees had a hard time from the spectators. Distington and Pica Athletic won many trophies. Pica were the league winners in 1927. At an Annual General Meeting held in June, 1930, Pica Athletic were in debt and struggled throughout the season. It was decided to close down the club.

Distington played on a pitch at Bankside until the flat top houses were built there in 1942. The pitch for Distington AFC was moved to the Barffs, beside the Lime Road. Another pitch was laid out in a field above the HDA. This pitch had quite a big slope. Part of the Lillyhall Industrial Factories estate is now on this site. Distington AFC won the Infirmary Cup in the 1944/45 season with a team organised by Bob Hodgson and Tom Blamire. This was when Jimmy Riddick learnt his skills as a centre forward.

A team was set up for the Distington Boy's Club by Sammy Glassford. Requiring a new strip, he wrote to Glasgow Celtic FC. They supplied everything, all the kit that was necessary. The team played on a field beside Barffs Quarry, shared with Distington AFC and the Rugby League team, when it was formed in 1951. They used the Black Lion and the British Legion as changing rooms but later had a green hut beside the pitch. The pitch became over-used and became a mud heap. It was known as 'The Midden'. Towards the end of a match, a group of men and boys would take a zinc bath, kept in the hut, to the Long Quarry, which was near to the pitch. The bath was filled with water from the quarry and carried back to the pitch for the boys to wash in. The quality of the water left much to be desired.

When National Service men returned home in the late 1940s, it was said that they were too old to rejoin the Boy's Club so they decided to form their own team, the Distington Corinthians. The organising committee consisted of Tom Blamire (Senior), Billy Steel, Tom Williamson and Andy Musgrave. The players were: A Williams, Ash Williams, Bill Mateer, Eric Warrilow, George Fraser (g k.) C Hewitt, G Myers, W Fleming, Derek Bell, Nick Williamson, Jim Halley, Jimmy Riddick, J (Skid) Townsley, Ron Shillito, Alec Allen, Donald Kirkpatrick and Bill Little. The team was trained by George Dick, who was at that time the Workington Reds captain and an ex-Blackpool AFC player.

When the strip was required for this team, Billy Steel wrote to Sunderland AFC and was supplied by a full kit of red and white striped shirts and black shorts. The team trained in the Victoria Hall. Being very fit men, the team won every competition they took part in. They won the Derwent Valley League, the Payne Cup, the League Cup, the Workington Knock-out Cup and the Infirmary Shield over a period of five years.

At this time, HDA and the British Legion also ran teams in the winter and summer Leagues. A number of players turned out for more than one side. Tony Rosser, who normally played for HDA was persuaded to play for Distington AFC. In his first game, he broke his leg and never played again.

A Workington Sunday League playing for the Legion in 1964 consisted of: Brian Halley, Keith Hunter, Bob Bedford (Senior), Brian Sutton, George Messenger, Brian Messenger, Peter Donnelly, Alan Denwood goalkeeper, John Gallagher, Brian Riddick and John Manduell. Keith Hunter was killed in the North Sea Oil Rig disaster in July 1988 and Peter Donnelly later played professional Rugby League for Whitehaven RLFC.

Few changes were made to the team. Jimmy Redding also played some games as goalkeeper until was injured. After this, he then played as a winger. The team played ten matches, winning nine and losing only one, scoring 80 goals with only 20 against. Bob Bedford, (Senior), played, coached and managed a number of teams. He retired from playing football when he was 54 and died when he was 59.

One of the best teams of the 60s played in the Sunday League Challenge Cup Final at the Borough Park Football Ground, Workington, on Saturday 1st May 1966. The FA did not allow grounds to be used on a Sunday at that time. The team was: - Goalkeeper-Alan Denwood, full-backs John Gallagher and Mickey Burns, half-backs Albert Linford, Geoff Richardson and Brian Sutton, forwards Ron Bedford and his twin brother Rob, Bob Taylor (Capt) Bobby Pickering and John Manduell. Brian Kennett and Alan Corlett were

Distington AFC 1967/1968

WORKINGTON AND DISTRICT AMATEUR
SUNDAY ASSOCIATION FOOTBALL
LEAGUE

Challenge Cup Final 1967-1968

DISTINGTON

versus

ELLIOTT BROS. F.C.
(Maryport)

BOROUGH PARK, WORKINGTON

SATURDAY, 11th MAY, 1968

Kick-off 6 p.m.

Admission by Programme 1/-

DISTINGTON

Colours: White Shirts, Blue Shorts.

A. Denwood

M. Burns

R. Corlett

B. Sutton

J. Cowan   B. Messenger

G. Hewer

R. Taylor (capt.)

Ron Bedford   Rob Bedford   J. Manduell

Substitute: R. PICKERING

Referee—Mr. A. MURPHY.

Linesmen: Mr. I. TAYLOR and Mr. A. CROSS.

Substitute: T. HODGSON.

W. Smith   A. Timney   G. Hooper

A. Wilson

B. Renney

F. Martin

J. Oakes (capt.)   G. Wilson

G. Johnstone

K. Ivison

D. Hymers

Colours: All Blue.

ELLIOTT BROS. F.C.

---

reserves. Distington won 2 - 1, with goals by Rob Bedford and Brian Sutton. In the Sunday League County Cup, Distington beat Carlisle Post-Office Engineers 3 - 0, but lost the next game to Carlisle Wrestlers at Cockermouth 1 - 3.

In the 66/67 season, Distington won the league comfortably with HDA finishing fifth. In the two games against each other, Distington won 6 goals to 1 and then 8 goals to 2. During this season, before a match against Elliott Bros of Maryport, Secretary Bob Bedford received a phone call to say that Elliott Bros team could not raise a team and the match was off. However, at the required time, Elliott's and the referee turned up but not Distington, so Elliott's claimed the match. At the following inquiry, Elliott's Bros denied making the call so the match was played during the midweek. Distington won easily. In another match against Elliott Bros, the referee abandoned the game after sending off an Elliott's player and the team refused to play on.

The season of 67/68 was a very good year. Distington AFC played 26 games in league and cup competitions, winning every match. They scored 157 goals with just 22 against. Their biggest win was 15 - 2 with two games at 13 - 0. The following season 1968/69, Distington played 15 League games winning twelve with two games drawn and lost only one, their first defeat for 18 months. Three teams did not bother to turn up for their match, giving Distington the points on a walkover. They scored 80 goals for, with 17 against. Rob Bedford was the League's leading marksman. Distington were a very successful team.

In a special match, a British Legion side played the Rector's side to raise money for the church. The Legion won 9 - 8. £30-00 was collected. The British Legion team consisted of J Hulmes, J Blamyre, J Flynn, T Bateman, Bob Bedford, (Senior), T Clarke, F Fields, Jimmy Riddick, George Messenger, Mick Ferguson and B Thompson. In the Rector's team were Ron Wilson, Ronnie Rogerson, R Southard, F Brown, John Calvert, G Beck, John Lace, Nick Williamson, Rev. Bill Kelly, Ron Shillito and T Tremble. Matt Penney was the trainer, J Hunter was the referee and Ron Butler was a linesman.

Distington still had a successful Sunday League football team in the 1980s. Some boys approached Ernie Hewer in 1980 and a new team was formed for the 1981/82 season. Ernie became player/

manager, making him a player over three decades and Raymond Porter assisted him.

They played on the pitch at Lillyhall School. In the 1983/84 season, they achieved the Grand Slam, winning the Sunday County Cup, plus the three main Workington Sunday League competitions, the President's Cup, Premier League and the League Cup. Those involved in the team were Ernie Hewer, player/manager, Richard Hewer, Paul Hunter, David George, Ken Mason, Steve Sutton, Raymond Porter, Gary Ireland, Stephen Hodgson, Stephen Martin, Stephen Seeds, Keith Glover, Chris Kelly, Paul and Gary Messenger, Ian, Terry and Craig Adams, Dave McKenzie and Billy Monan. Paul Hewer was the club mascot. All of the team were Distington lads except three. Most of the team played rugby league on the Saturday and football on the Sunday. Their fitness and teamwork gave them their success.

Distington won the President's Cup by beating Flimby 4–2, after being 0-2 at half time. They then beat the Cumberland Star team 2-1 in the Sunday League Cup Final at Borough Park in 1985. Those taking part in the team were Ernie Hewer, Stephen Martin, Ian Adams, Chris Kelly, Steve Sutton, Richard Hewer, Billy Monan, Dave McKenzie, Gary Ireland, Paul Messenger, Gary Messenger, Keith Glover and Stephen Hodgson. This team lost only one game, to Silloth, who were relegated that year.

Distington at this time also had a Boy's Club team in the under 16s competitions. It was led by Eddie Neen, Frank Farr and Ron Wilson. They won their cup with a 3-0 win over Mirehouse. The team was Andrew Martin, Paul Davidson, Neil Daniels, Chris Stables, Ian Clark, Sean Ennis, Gary Hewer, Ken and James Milligan, Chris Dempster, Paul Richardson, Carl Henderson and Ian Kirkbride.

A Distington man, Robin Sharpe, has been involved in local football for most of his life. He retired at the end of the 2007 season after being a player, referee and linesman for more than 1,000 games. Robin was playing as a mid field player when he was recommended to become a referee. He became a Grade Five referee and took control of games in the Workington and District Sunday League, the Egremont League, the County League and the old Northern League, based in the north east. He has also acted as referee in women's matches. To keep fit he walked 25 to 30 miles a week and has run in 12

London marathons. He took charge of his first game at the Marchon ground at Kells. During this game a player committed a foul and was penalised for it. He did not accept the decision so he was sent off. Robin did not like booking players but a referee has to keep control. He retired after 43 years, aged 75.

High Duty Alloys Teams
A report by Tony Rosser.

HDA also played in the same Derwent Valley League as Distington AFC. Throughout the 1960s, Brian Kennet, Brian Sutton, Bobby Taylor and Bob Bedford (Junior) all played for HDA and Distington AFC in the then popular Sunday League. Matches were played to the north of the HDA factory a pitch of a notorious slope, now the site of a factory on the Lillyhall estate. In the early days the pitch sloped down from the Distington to Cockermouth road towards the old slag banks, but was recreated to run parallel with the A595 road. Teams no longer had to play uphill or downhill. In 1965, HDA Sports were very fortunate to be presented with a new football pitch and clubhouse, built in 1969 and was complete with full changing room facilities. A cricket pitch and a hockey pitch were also laid out. A hockey team became second to none in Cumberland and a number of players went on to play for England. After WWII, hard surface tennis courts had been built, adjacent to the British Road Services depot to the north of the HDA works and opposite the junction with the high road to Workington.

Although impressive in its appearance and no expense was spared on the facilities, the drainage of the pitch was not good. It was compared with the old muddy Barffs Quarry pitch.

Due to the well-stocked Saturday team in 1966, the junior players, the nucleus being HDA apprentices, were unable to get a game. No subs were allowed in those days. With this in mind, the Sunday League team was developed as a second team for the main HDA Saturday team. It was formed in 1965 and took the name of the High Duty Alloys United. Although it never had huge success, it played its part. Some notable players were developed for the Saturday team. Jack Seeds was an ever-present throughout its 10 year existence with Tony Rosser defecting to Distington, be it for just one game in 1971.

RUGBY LEAGUE

When Northern Union Football came to the village, Bob Stephenson, a Distington man, was capped to play for the County. Northern Union later became Rugby League. Distington had a number of teams through the years, including school teams in a local league. The school played regularly against Moresby Parks, Lowca and Parton schools.

The following is from the memories and records of the late Bob Coulton, a very fine player in his day of the team set up after WW II.

When Rugby League ended at the HDA, a few villagers brought in Mr G Plummer and Mr T Banks, chairman, of the Cumberland Commissioners and Mr Tyson, secretary of the British Amateur Rugby League Association, known as BARLA. A special meeting was called at the Distington British Legion with a view to forming a new team for Distington. A committee was formed at this meeting. Mr Packy Newton became President, T Clark became chairman, Bob Coulton vice chairman, Bill Foster, secretary and Alan McSherry treasurer. The committee consisted of Arthur Dempster, R Southard, Mr and Mrs Dawson of the Queens Head, Mrs Kelly, Mrs Morrison, Packy Hunter and D Crone. The Queens Head was the Headquarters. The Victoria Hall was used to hold whist drives and other entertainments to bring in funds. The playing field was Brigg's field, at the junction of the Pica road and the Loop Road and to the rear of Millyard.

Bob Coulton

The rugby league committee organised a competition in the Enterprise Ballroom to elect the Distington Rugby League Queen, won by Ivy Watson. The judges were Tony Paskins and John Mudge, two players who had just arrived from Australia to play for Workington Rugby League team. Mr and Mrs Newton were the hosts for the evening and this brought in enough money to pay for a new strip from the Gus Risman Sports shop. Eric Thomas, the school sports master, joined in to mark out the new pitch. In return, the school also used this pitch for their matches. The village squire,

Austin Robertson-Walker kindly gave permission to cut six suitable trees for the goal posts, from his estate, also helping us to cut them to the correct size. Transport of these posts was carried out by coal merchant Ernie Lamb, free of charge. The team played its first game in 1951.

Notable players to come through these teams were John Roper, Workington Town RLFC and George Killen, both from Pica. George played for Whitehaven RLFC and Huddersfield RLFC. He also played for Australia after emigrating. He was killed in Kenya, fighting as a mercenary against the Mau-Mau.

In 1982, Frank Hewer noticed that schoolchildren had nowhere to play except on the streets. After talking to other people, he decided that the area at the end of Hinnings Road, a lonning and seven narrow fields, known as Grass Road by Copeland Council and locally as Hall Flats, would make a suitable ground. Hall Road was owned by the Northern Housing Association, later the Home Housing, who had planned to build houses on the playing field. In 1982, word came through that these building plans had been dropped. Hall Flats was a neglected area and a rubbish dump.

A new committee was formed on 24th June 1984, two years after the first discussions took place. Minutes of the meetings reported that the following men were elected into office.

Chairman was John Manduell, Hon Secretary was Frank Hewer and the Hon Treasurer was Neil Hewer. Others who attended and became committee members were Joe Hewer, Manny Stalker, Gordon and Ron Hewer, and John Davidson. Albert Linford and Dick Crawford both had agreed before the meeting that they were willing to help out and were voted on in their absence. They formed the Distington Amateur Rugby League Club. John Davidson proved to be a driving force on this project.

A letter was sent to Copeland Council, making enquiries about the ground. The answer was that no funds were available to develop the ground. The committee then set about fund raising. A carnival was set up in the Pond Field, ran for a number of years and gave plenty of fun. Fancy dress competitions and a pram race proved to be very popular. These races stopped in 1992, not because of lack of entries but because prams became unavailable. The first games were to be friendly matches, played away from home until a pitch was found. The first pitch used was at Lillyhall School, loaned until 1987, but in later years became a quagmire.

Changes to the committee took place in 1985. John Manduell moved to become Treasurer and Joe Hewer became Chairman. Grants were given by Copeland Council of £30,000 for the pitch at Grass Road. More money was raised by Bob Milligan, Bill Marsh and Neil Hewer, with a lot of help from the committee member's wives. A raffle was held, selling 200 tickets, once a fortnight. Prizes were donated by local business companies. Hensingham Amateur Rugby League (A.R.L) Club gave a set of their strip, red shirts with a white collar, to Distington. They also staged the first friendly game so another kit had to be borrowed to avoid the colour clash. This game was played on 24th July 1984. Myers and Bowman's lent the club a van to take them to play at Haverigg against the H M Prison team. They lost both these friendly games. In August 1984, John Davis joined the committee and in September 1984 was appointed coach. Bill McKenzie, landlord of the Globe Hotel, became the Club President.

In March 1985, the club bought a 40 foot long trailer from Egremont Tubes. This was placed into position where the new club rooms stand today. The wheel base was removed and given to Tyson Burridge in exchange for a new kit. The cost of the trailer and expenses came to £340. To make it into club rooms, partition walls were put in and windows were cut into the sides. Joe Bennett acquired five old baths and four old electric boilers. On match days, Frank and Joe Hewer would carry water from the house of Mary Towers of Hinnings Road, which had already been pre-heated. This was paid for by giving a bag of coal and £2.00. Near the end of playing time, the boilers were used to heat up the water to the required level. The electricity came from Joe Burn's house in Hinnings Road. A contribution was made for the cost of the electric power. They used this arrangement all through the 1985/86 season.

A new club house was built, starting in September 1985 and completed by May 1986. The finance came from Jennings Brewery. A drinking licence was granted and the social side developed to give a steady income. This club became the Sports and Social club. The changing rooms and pitches belong to Copeland Council.

All this came about because Frank wanted somewhere for the school children to play in safety. He did not set out to form a rugby club.

This team unfortunately folded in 2003. Another group was then set up by Gary Hewer, starting from scratch and based in the Globe Hotel. They were admitted to the West Cumbrian Amateur League for the start of the 2005 season.

John (Sol) Roper

This record of John's playing career is by courtesy of the Workington News & Star.

The best known player in the parish was John (Sol) Roper, born in Pica in 1936. He played professional Rugby League for both Workington and Whitehaven. As a schoolboy in the early 1950s, he played for Distington School against other local school sides. He captained Cumberland Schoolboys team in 1951.

After schooldays, Sol played for Distington and Hensingham as an amateur and was picked for the England Open Age team when he was 17. He scored a try in England's win over France on 17th April 1954. Sol then had a trial with Whitehaven but was told he was too small to make the grade. He moved to Workington and was soon in the first team as a professional. He made his debut in August 1954, aged 18, in a win over Featherstone. Two weeks later he made his county debut for Cumberland against Yorkshire. He became the regular scrum-half for Workington Town Rugby League team but was often the smallest man on the pitch, tackling players much bigger than him.

In the Challenge Cup in 1955, Town went to Wembley, playing against Barrow. Sol was the youngest player on the pitch. Barrow won 21-12. Three years later, Town again got to Wembley. This time, Sol was captain, the youngest captain at that time and again the youngest man on the pitch. Workington lost this match to Wigan in May 1958 by 13-9. One week later they again lost in the Championship Play-off Final in Bradford. In all three games, injuries changed the course of the

Sol Roper introducing his team at Wembley to His Excellency, Mr J H Whitney, USA Ambassador to UK.
Photograph by permission of Sol Roper and Workington News & Star.

game. Sol eventually got his winner's medal in 1962, in the Western Division Championship Final at Wigan, beating Widnes after a replay. He was the only man to have been captain in both major competitions. Sol's last game for Workington was in a second round cup match on 19th March 1966, having played 385 times for the club.

A year later, he went on loan to Whitehaven, playing his first game in Nov 1967. He was there for five years and played 82 times, finishing as player-coach. His last game for Whitehaven was at Widnes on 27th February 1972. His last game for Cumberland was at Derwent Park Workington, against Yorkshire played on the 1st October 1969. He had played 21 times for his county. In his total career, he played 502 times, scored 110 tries and kicked 10 goals giving him a total of 350 points. Sol's son, Tony played professional Rugby League for Workington in his time and his grandson Jonathon, played for Warrington at the turn of the century and has now returned to Workington Town.

CRICKET

A Cricket Club was organised and played on the flat ground behind the old Rectory. The Rectory grounds were the regular venue. The first match was on 26th August 1882. The Club ran successfully for nearly 60 years until the ground was taken over for the building of the houses in Glebe Road in 1942. A large oak tree used to stand outside number 13 Kilnside. There was a notice board nailed to the tree advertising the cricket ground. No other ground existed again until the HDA Sports Club and ground was built at Lillyhall. The club was dissolved before the West Lakes College was built. A new cricket team plays in the village today to keep the tradition going.

BILLIARDS

Between the wars, the Reading Room had a successful billiards team. They won the West

Cumberland League, the Whitehaven and District Cup and the Whitehaven and District Shield. After WW II, the billiard and snooker teams played in the British Legion. They had successful teams for many years.

HOUND TRAILING.

Hound Trailing was and still is a popular sport in the area, usually well attended by local people and farmers, who give permission to run on their fields. The sport is controlled by the Hound Trailing Association, started by a Whitehaven man in 1906. The Hound Trailing Association (HTA) has now spread out over other counties and also across to Ireland. Cumbria is split into 7 sections, with Whitehaven covering West Cumbria. Distington man Henry Ward is on the HTA Committee. Breeding has produced a strong dog, capable of overcoming rough conditions on the fells.

Harriet Beatty, of the Black Cock pub Distington, was a keen breeder of dogs. She organised race meetings starting from the field at the rear of the pub. The season ranges from April to October. Three trails usually take place. Hounds, puppies and open restricted races for dogs that have not won more than four races. Hound dog owners would meet at the Black Cock for a drink before racing started. Ronnie Rogerson of Main Street, who was well known for his work at Myers and Bowman's, was an organiser of trails as well as an owner. John Lace (senior) and his son, also called John of Pandora Terrace, laid the scents for the dogs to follow. Each would start from the centre point of the trail, one laying the scent to the start of the race and the other laid the trail to the finish. The hound owners met up for meetings at the Queens Head pub. John Ward of Beck Green was a well known racer and breeder of dogs, as was Caddy Ward. Jimmy Crone of Hinnings Road was another man well known for his knowledge of dogs.

PIGEON RACING

Bob McAvoy of Common End supplied the following information.

Pigeon racing has taken place over many years in the village. At the turn of the 20th century, only one clock existed for racing. This was at the school

in the Main St. Pigeon owners at Furnace Row and Common End complained about the unfair advantage that the owners in the middle of the village had. Now all lofts have their own clocks.

Distington had a Homing Society with plenty of members. In 1964, members were listed as Ward Brothers, Larry, John and Joe of Beck Green, Johnny Mossop and Bill Stephenson, John Mason of Main Street, Tom Hewer and son, Frank, Bob Crone Senior with his son also called Bob of the Globe Hotel and his brother Dick, Archie and Albert Wilkinson, of Chapel Street, Tom Taylor, of Hinnings Road, Henry Allen and son Alec, of Kilnside, George Reay and sons, Lennie Penrice and Ronnie Butler, Dennis Hodgson, John McAvoy and Alan Teare, John Kennett and son Brian, and Billy Allan and his son.

Distington was one of 12 Homing Societies, (some were called Flying Clubs), which formed the West Cumberland Federation, known as The Fed. The Fed covered an area from Lillyhall and Lowca in the north, Lamplugh Church tower in the east, Silecroft in the south and was based in Whitehaven. The Fed was in turn part of the Royal National Homing Union and Federations. Three members were enough to form a club. Each loft was given a measured distance in miles and yards from Silecroft. This was added to the distance of the race from its starting point to Silecroft, giving each loft an equal chance of winning. For example, the distance from Silecroft to the loft of J Kennett and son was 27 miles 479 yards. A & A Wilkinson's distance was given as 26 miles 1628 yards. The time was then worked out for each bird's flight, recorded from the time of the bird's release at the beginning of the race, to its arrival at its own loft. A numbered ring was taken from the leg of each bird and locked into a clock box. The timer stopped when the box was locked.

In 1964, races were started from Lancaster, 24 miles 1166 yards to Silecroft, Leyland 45 miles 107 yards, Newton-le-Willows 61 miles 568 yards, Nantwich 87 miles 222 yards, Shrewsbury 107 miles 886 yards, Cannock 119 miles 861 yards, Worcester 148 miles 106 yards, Cheltenham 169 miles 142 yards, Christchurch 249 miles 1610 yards, St Malo, France 389 miles 1604 yards, Dol, France 398 miles 1147 yards, Rennes, France 429 miles 320 yards and Nantes, France 491 miles 886 yards. Young birds had their own races but never flew over the Channel. Their longest distance was from Christchurch.

Five Prizes and Trophies were awarded during the racing season. The Federation Cup was awarded to the winner of the first Christchurch race. The Boy's Club Trophy was awarded for the Christchurch Yearling race, with cash specials for the first three birds. This was only given to those clubs that had donated to the Cumberland and Westmorland Association of Boy's Clubs. Cash prizes of £3, £2 and £1 were given for the first three birds in the Rennes race. The Patterson Cup was for the winner of the Nantes race. A bottle of rum was donated by Matthew Brown And Company to the winner Rennes race. The Adams Memorial Trophy and Mini Cup went to the winner of the Dol race. Entry fees was 6d, (2½p) per bird.

Young birds raced for the Hospital Cup in the first Worcester race. Entry fee was 1 shilling (5p) per bird. Ten pounds was given for the best average of all three French races. All trophies were competed for on an annual basis.

1964 was the last year that trains were used to transport the pigeons. After that a wagon supplied by H Pickthall of Cleator Moor, carried the racers. Each driver was accompanied by a conveyor to look after and to water the birds and release them at the required time. The Fed now has its own vehicle.

Forty years later, many changes have taken place. Today, the Distington Homing Society has only five members, Bob McAvoy, Secretary of the club, Jack Allen, John Turner, John Harrison and John Barnes. John Turner is Distington representative on the Fed Committee.

The Federation has also changed. Some clubs have gone while others have started up. Eleven clubs now form the Federation. Racing still takes place every weekend during the season. Now, old birds fly from Burscough, Appleton, Salford, Woolaton, Cheltenham, Newbury and Fareham in England. From France, they race from Vire, Fougeres and Nantes. Young birds still do not fly from France and their first race is from Garstang. Their longest race is from Ventnor, Isle of Wight.

The Silecroft breaking point is no longer used. Today's breaking point is at the Pelican Garage Whitehaven, but for open races, a 'Great Circle' is measured from the starting point to each loft. The young bird winner in the Cheltenham race receives the Myers and Bowman's Cup, plus the BNFL Shield. The pigeons are expected to fly from 40 mph to 70 mph according to winds and weather. Long distance flights can take six to eight hours of non-stop flying. Pigeon breeders sell birds for £50 but the world record is £132,000. Because of these costs, loft owners are reluctant to fly these birds. Sparrow hawks have become a big problem now so the sport is slowly dying out.

ACKNOWLEDGEMENTS

Thanks to:

Ron Shillito, for the use of his Mannix and Whellan directory of 1847 and also for his photographs

John Lamb, for the use of his Bulmer's directory of 1883

Rev J Stagg, for permission to use the Church Centenary book,

The Cumberland and Westmorland Antiquarian Society for permission to use information from the book by the late Oliver Wood on Cumberland Mining 1600 – 1982,

The late Gilbert Rothery for information on High Duty Alloys Ltd.,

The late Maurice Boyd and his son, Michael for their information of Myers & Bowman's, Motor Engineers,

Margaret Ogilvy, for her information of J S Crookdake's Smithy and Garage,

Cissie Tinnion for information on the Boy's Club and the School Centenary book,

John Marr of Mitchell's Auctions Ltd for information of Gilgarran Hall

Alan Denwood, for extracts from his scrap book on Distington AFC football,

Henry Ward and Frank Hewer for their information of Distington ARL

Nora Lace for her assistance in the Record Office

For the use of photographs, I thank my wife Ethel, who took the modern photographs and spent many hours in the Whitehaven Record Office with me and to the Record Office staff for their help,

For the loan of their photographs, I thank Margaret Ogilvy, Michael Boyd and his sister Jan Relph, Cissie Tinnion, Russell and Stuart Grant, Nora Lace and Margaret Steele. I thank the Times & Star Newspaper, Workington. The Whitehaven News and the Barrow Mail, for the photograph by Roger Savage, and the Workington Library for use of their photographs.

Also, thanks to Maureen Fisher and to John Garner for their advice, to Colin Denwood for his expertise on the computer and last but not least, to my many friends and neighbours in the village who gave me so much valuable information.

Every effort has been made to credit photographs used in this publication. If we have missed anyone please accept our apologies.

About the author

I was born on Coronation Day of King George VI and Queen Elizabeth, 12th May 1937, in Slough, then in Buckinghamshire. My family moved to West Cumberland when my dad was transferred from H D A Slough to Distington in 1941. We lived for two years at 6 Cambridge Road, Hensingham, before moving to 3 Gilgarran View in August 1943. After 18 months at Hensingham School, I spent the remainder of my school years at Distington Secondary Modern school, leaving in 1952.

I started work at the North Western Electricity Board, Whitehaven as a apprentice electrician and completed my apprenticeship in 1958. Then came two years National Service in the Royal Engineers. On my return, I worked another two years at NWEB, Whitehaven before being transferred to Workington. It was here that I started working on street lighting maintenance, which became my job for the rest of my working life.

In 1965, I moved to Workington Corporation until local government changes on 1st April 1974. I was then transferred to Cumbria County Council. In June 1974, I got married to Ethel. I now have three daughters, four grandsons and four granddaughters and now two great grand children.

My next move was on 1st December 1975 when I went to work for the London Borough of Hounslow in a supervising role. The 3,000 street lights I had maintained at Workington became 25,000, including the A4 Great West Road, part of the M4 motorway and later, part of the M25 motorway.

I retired in 1993 because of health reasons and returned to live in Distington. A History Society was set up in the Community Centre which led to my present interest in local history.